KEY
WORDS
of the
CHRISTIAN
FAITH

Also by Reinder Bruinsma:

Matters of Life and Death
Faith—Step by Step

To order, call 1-800-765-6955.

Visit us at
www.reviewandherald.com
for information on other Review and Herald® products.

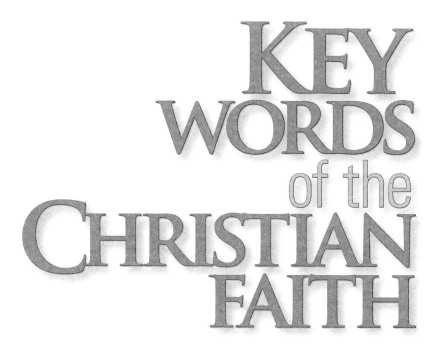

KEY WORDS of the CHRISTIAN FAITH

REINDER BRUINSMA

REVIEW AND HERALD® PUBLISHING ASSOCIATION
Since 1861 | www.reviewandherald.com

Published by Review and Herald® Publishing Association, Hagerstown, MD 21741-1119

Review and Herald® titles may be purchased in bulk for educational, business, fund-raising, or sales promotional use. For information, please e-mail SpecialMarkets@reviewandherald.com.

The Review and Herald® Publishing Association publishes biblically based materials for spiritual, physical, and mental growth and Christian discipleship.

The author assumes full responsibility for the accuracy of all facts and quotations as cited in this book.

Unless otherwise noted, Scripture quotations in this book are taken from the *Holy Bible,* New Living Translation, copyright © 1996. Used by permission of Tyndale House Publishers, Inc., Wheaton, Illinois 60189. All rights reserved.

Texts credited to NIV are from the *Holy Bible, New International Version.* Copyright © 1973, 1978, 1984, International Bible Society. Used by permission of Zondervan Bible Publishers.

Bible texts credited to RSV are from the Revised Standard Version of the Bible, copyright © 1946, 1952, 1971, by the Division of Christian Education of the National Council of the Churches of Christ in the U.S.A. Used by permission.

This book was
Edited by Gerald Wheeler
Copyedited by James Cavil
Designed by Ron J. Pride
Cover photo © Photodisc
Interior design by Heather Rogers
Typeset: Bembo 12/14

PRINTED IN U.S.A.

12 11 10 09 08   5 4 3 2 1

Library of Congress Cataloging-in-Publication Data
Bruinsma, Reinder.
  Key words of the Christian faith / Reinder Bruinsma.
     p. cm.
  1. Christianity—Terminology. 2. Theology, Doctrinal. I. Title.
  BR96.5.B78 2008
  230—dc22
                              2008013916

ISBN 978-0-8280-2340-5

DEDICATED

to all my Adventist colleagues
in ministry
in the Netherlands

CONTENTS

PREFACE

The story is told that during a visit to the Theological Department of the University of Chicago Karl Barth, the famous German theologian, held a press conference. One journalist asked him, "If you were asked to summarize the essence of the Christian faith, what would you, after your long career of Bible study, say?" Students of theology have often been greatly dismayed at the density of much of Barth's writings, but on this occasion there was nothing complicated about what he said. Without missing a beat, he replied: "What it all boils down to is this: Jesus loves me, this I know. For the Bible tells me so!"*

Maybe that is also all I should say. For any attempts at summarizing the essence of the Christian faith are, in a certain sense, doomed to fail. The Christian faith is so deep and rich that no book can do justice to it. Human minds must humbly admit that God and His plan of salvation are truths of an order that human reasoning and finite language cannot adequately deal with. Yet in His grace God has revealed enough to us to enable us to establish a meaningful relationship with Him, and He invites us to continue mining His Word for treasures so that we may steadily "grow in grace" (2 Peter 3:18, KJV). Therefore, trying to encapsulate some of the key elements of our faith may have a useful purpose. It may bring out some aspects that some of us have not thought about before and may help us to see some things just a bit clearer.

When I sat down to write the *Adult Sabbath School Bible Study Guide* lessons about key words of the Christian faith, I was, by the very fact that such a guide must consist of only 13 studies, limited in the number of key words that I could choose. I would have liked to include one or two other vital concepts. The final choices are, admittedly, rather subjective. As I prepared this companion book I had to follow the pattern of the *Bible Study Guide*—with, again, the same limitations.

It might have been easier to write a little book about each of the 13 topics than to restrict myself to less than an average of 4,000 words for each concept. Each chapter could touch upon only a few aspects. Readers will notice that I tend to ask many questions. I hope some of these will inspire them toward further study. I hope, though, that I have succeeded also in showing that, in spite of all the questions that often baffle us, we do have some solid answers that give us a firm foundation for our faith.

Writing this book has, once again, forced me to do some intense and structured thinking about my faith as a Seventh-day Adventist Christian. I have considered it a privilege to work on this. I pray many will not only find themselves encouraged to ask questions but also find answers and experience the glorious assurance of salvation.

I have used the New Living Translation throughout this book. The reason is not that I have made a careful evaluation of all available Bible translations in the English language and have concluded that it is definitely better than any other. I have recently, however, discovered this translation as a version that I (whose native language is not English) find very clear and fresh. Listening to the way in which the translators have rendered the text, I often hear things and nuances that I have not noticed before. My hope and prayer is that this book will give—at least to some—fresh insights to those who read it and contemplate their faith.

Reinder Bruinsma
Hoevelaken, Netherlands

---

* I first read this story in Philip Yancey, *What's So Amazing About Grace?* (Grand Rapids: Zondervan Pub. House), p. 97.

LOVE 1

All you need is love." More than 40 years have gone by since the four young men from the British city of Liverpool first sang this famous line. Even today's postmodern generation knows the words, and whenever something reminds people of the Beatles, this lyric pops up. It has been played, sung, hummed, downloaded, and listened to on the radio by hundreds of millions of young and not-so-young men and women around the world. But how many have stopped to give some careful thought to the words? Are they actually true? Can love indeed take care of all our needs? Will we be able to meet whatever challenges might come our way as long as we have love in our lives? Is love the only essential element for a happy and satisfying existence?

If the frequency of its use determined its place on the ladder of meaning, the word "love" would have a good chance of coming out on top. Or maybe not quite. Possibly the word "sex" and related terms would score even higher. That would certainly apply if we were to include our unspoken thoughts with the words that actually pass our lips. Researchers suggest that the average male in our Western world thinks about sex in one form or another once every 52 seconds. Women apparently are not quite as sex-obsessed as men, but their minds also frequently turn to the subject of sex (on the average, in their fertile period, at least a few times a day). Maybe we cannot fully substantiate such claims, but for many the words "love" and "sex" are almost interchangeable, and when they repeat the words credited to John Lennon and Paul McCartney ("All you need is love") they really mean "All you need (and want) is sex."

An immense amount of confusion surrounds the topic of love and much of what has the love label so casually attached to it does not deserve that name. Often, what many call love is, indeed, no more than lust and an unrestrained craving for sex in endless variety. Often it has nothing, or very little, to do with genuine feeling and true attachment, and everything to do with the self-centered gratification of urges constantly reinforced by the media and popular culture. In many cases, love is just about *me*—*my* power, *my* possessions, *my* drives, *my* goals and ambitions—and about nothing else.

Love in the divine scheme of things

I do not know how much the Beatles knew of the Bible or about religion when they sang "All You Need Is Love" and whether they realized that their words voiced a religious truth of crucial importance. For these few words oddly echo what one of the great founders of Christendom, the apostle Paul, wrote to the believers in the Greek city of Corinth. He short-listed the basic ingredients of true Christian life: faith, hope, and love. In many of his writings he emphasizes the importance of having *faith*. Faith in Christ Jesus is a condition for being saved (Rom. 1:17). He also wants there to be no misunderstanding about the vital role of *hope* in the experience of the Christian (2 Tim. 1:12). But, when all is said and done, there is nothing more important than *love* (1 Cor. 13:13). Yes, Paul says, "All you need is love." Everything else is, in fact, wrapped up in the package of true Christian love.

Even though Paul speaks about love in the famous thirteenth chapter of his First Epistle to the Corinthians in words that have inspired millions of Christ's disciples through the centuries, the substance of what he wrote was not something totally new. His Lord stated the same principle when He told His followers: "You must love the Lord your God with all your heart, all your soul, all your mind, and all your strength" (Mark 12:30). And even Christ was not totally original in what He said. He was, in fact, simply quoting some ancient wording from the Old Testament (Deut. 6:5).

Many people who have very little knowledge of the Bible, are nonetheless able to quote the famous love text from the third chapter of the Gospel of John. It is probably the best known and most cited Bible verse: "For God so loved the world that he gave his only Son, so that everyone who believes in him will not perish but have eternal life" (verse 16). And many will also remember the final words of another oft-quoted Bible text: "*God is love*" (1 John 4:8). Nothing rates higher on the divine scale of values than love.

God's love comes first

Without any doubt love is the absolute key word in the Christian's vocabulary. But let's be sure to get things in the correct order. Scripture tells us that to be a true follower of Christ, we must love God with all our heart, soul, and intellect (Mark 12:30). In other words, we must love with our entire being. How do we do that? Is this something that comes *naturally* to the Christian? Or can we *learn* how to love God? Do we somehow "catch" it by going to church, by watching religious broadcasts or listening to religious music as we drive our car to work? Or can the children who sing "Oh, how I love Jesus!" teach us a thing or two about this love?

From the outset we must keep one thing in mind: it is not the way in which humans love each other that informs us about what our love for God might be like. It is precisely the other way around. The way in which God loves us informs us about the manner in which we may respond to God's love. It gives all our human love a dimension it would not have if we were ignorant of divine love. Whatever love we may be able to generate, it is ultimately "a result of his first loving us" (1 John 4:19).

God's love differs from our love in that He loves infinitely, in-discriminately, unconditionally, and unselfishly. The Lord does not begin to love on the premise that there must be a response if He is

13

going to continue loving. He does not operate on the basis that He will love some of His creatures more than others, simply because some happen to be more lovable. Neither is His love subject to any sudden mood changes. "Long ago the Lord said to Israel: 'I have loved you, my people, with an everlasting love. With unfailing love I have drawn you to myself'" (Jer. 31:3). That's pretty strong language. And reassuring!

God loves in ways that we find impossible to understand. It is not a negotiated love. God does not say, "Listen, if you are nice to Me, I will love you." God loved us already when we were not yet around, but were present only in His unlimited divine database as creatures He knew that He would one day give the breath of life. He now loves us while we live our short life on earth, whether we seek Him or reject Him. And He continues loving us when we sleep the slumber of death and are safe in His memory. It is the kind of love reflected in Jesus' love for His disciples. Christ showed His disciples "the full extent of his love" (John 13:1). That included also the one that He knew would soon betray Him. Jesus continued to love Judas. I wonder whether we might say that, in a way, God continues to love even the devil!

God's love is pure *gift love*. He gave His only son. His "unfailing love . . . came through Jesus Christ" (John 1:17). He so loved us that He gave . . . His gifts keep coming, unlimited and unrestricted. The Lord loves the universe and all those worlds that we know nothing about. He loves our world, Planet Earth. And even though He will eventually judge the world and will have to say "Sorry" to those who have said their final no to Him, His love does not stop. Even His judgment is not detached from His love, nor is it a reversal of it. And if, at times, He needs to be tough with us, it is only because He does not give up on us. For "the Lord disciplines those he loves" (Heb. 12:6). All his actions are wrapped in eternal love.

Human love with a divine edge

Whatever true love we are able to give, it "comes from God" (1 John 4:7). Thank God (literally) that we *can* love. God is love, and He made us in His image. God has designed and constructed us with the capacity to love as He does. This does not mean that our love can ever *equal* that of God. But it means that we can love in a way that *resembles* divine love. Our love is and remains finite, partial, temporal, imperfect. It cannot be compared with God's love. We should not even say that God's love is much greater than our love, because there is absolutely no comparison whatsoever between finite human beings and the love they are capable of and the one almighty, omniscient, omnipresent, holy, perfect God and His love. Nonetheless, our love, however imperfect, can acquire a divine edge.

We love in different ways. The original language of the New Testament (Greek) uses four different words to express human love. *Agapē* is the highest kind of love. Scripture employs it for God's supreme love for us, and also uses it to express unselfish (or as unselfish as is humanly possible) human love toward God and toward a higher ideal. Other words express the love for our spouse—including sexual love—and our love for parents and children, for a friend, and for things. That in itself already indicates that we love in different ways and at different levels. But whatever love we are able to give, it must be touched by God's love if it is to be the kind of love that befits a follower of Christ. Let's look in a little more detail at the various forms of human love.

1. Loving your spouse. Of all relationships, the bond between (one) husband and (one) wife is the most wonderful. It originated in Paradise. The Creator embedded it in the fundamental social pattern that He imprinted on His creation. And it remains so precious that Scripture uses the relationship as a metaphor for the relation between Christ and His church. That in itself should warn us against the contemporary fashion in today's Western world of debunking marriage, or of regarding heterosexual marriage as just one option among a number of just-as-acceptable social models.

Finding a love partner for life—falling in love and staying in love "till death do us part"—is, apparently, far from easy. For the percentage of relationships that fail miserably and/or end in divorce is abysmally high. In the United States at least one third of all marriages end in divorce, and Europe is rapidly catching up. Even inside the church, divorce rates are nowadays not very much lower.

Why do so many marriages fail? One reason is that many enter marriage unprepared. Lots of people who tie the knot simply are not ready to assume the responsibilities that are part and parcel of marriage. Often they have not really asked themselves—or each other— the fundamental question of whether they are sufficiently compatible to live happily ever after. Tying the knot when you have very little in common is courting failure from the very beginning.

One of the most common reasons so many of our marriages do not last is that we base them on false expectations. We want our spouse to be near-perfect. The media bombard us with images of what the perfect partner should physically look like. And it is important that they do not just conform to the standards of what nowadays is considered beautiful or sexy on the wedding day. We also expect our spouse to remain attractive for many years to come—with or without Botox, face-lifts, and other surgical interventions. Our spouses should have prestigious, well-paying jobs, but also should be efficient in the work that needs to be done in and around the home. They must be innovative and untiring sexual partners. And, of course, our spouses need to be our friends and buddies, and, when the time has come to have children, perfect parents.

Not all of this is bad. Who would want to go back to the times that marriages were mostly business deals and people primarily sought and found romance in extramarital relationships? And what Western person wants to shift to a culture in which heads of the family still arrange marriages, or in which one may express the value of a prospective bride in a quantity of goats or cows? And in which the inability to produce offspring reduces the chances of marital success to virtually zilch.

By now do you see a pattern? People around us may refer to their relationships as *love* relationships, but what kind of love is it? In many cases it is not *gift love* but *take love* or *get love*. For many, their own needs come first. A failure to meet those needs leads to frustration and a lack of fulfillment. What is the use of continuing with a relationship, many will say, when you remain unfulfilled and your expectations do not get met? Why plod on, when the thought *Is this all there is to it?* keeps milling around in your head? Better quit and try again, before your chances are over!

Do you also see that in this type of relationship the divine edge is sadly missing? Unless the love for the spouse is primarily gift love, and unless both partners are intent on the happiness and fulfillment of the other, are looking for the true values that are more than skin-deep, and are not depending on what happens to be trendy, the chances that the relationship will survive is slim. The odds dramatically improve, however, when the love that God bestows upon us is reflected in the mutual love that we have discovered in our partner and in ourselves. Love with a divine edge is the ever-deepening love between me and the one person I intend to make happy, and who will, in turn, do everything to make me happy.

That kind of love will not be as everlasting as God's love, but it stands a good chance of enduring—especially when we are no longer in the prime of our life and we no longer emanate quite the same energy as we did on our wedding day. Whether or not Paul had any experience with married life, his words in Ephesians 5 still provide excellent counsel. "You wives will submit to your husbands as you do to the Lord" (verse 22). Read superficially, this hardly sounds like a directive one would like to repeat in the twenty-first century. But notice that we are not just talking about blind submission, as if we were still living two or three generations ago. Notice the way in which Paul qualifies such submission. We are discussing a relationship that is modeled after the relationship we enjoy with Christ. That is also expressed in the next piece of advice: "And you husbands must love your wives with the same love Christ showed the church" (verse 25). Both statements are basically saying the same thing: Bring God into your relationship (and keep Him in it). Faithfulness, forgiveness, and patience then become key factors in staying happy and overcoming the inevitable obstacles. You immediately and dramatically improve the chances that your relationship will be happy and enduring, as your love has taken on a divine edge.

2. *Loving your children and family/parents.* The state of the family in the Western world is not what it used to be. That is true even when we take into account the widespread tendency to believe that in the past most things, almost by definition, were better than they are today. During the twentieth century the average family became

smaller and gradually changed from a more extended family to a nuclear family of two generations—parents and their children. More recently our society has seen drastic changes. In many Western countries children now tend to live at home for a longer time than in the past. But that is not the most significant transformation. A huge percentage of families are one-parent families. Lots of children constantly shuttle back and forth between mother and father. Studies have estimated that divorce in some way affects roughly 60 percent of all children. The size of our social services continues to increase, as child abuse and spousal abuse demand record levels of attention.

It is no exaggeration to say that the family is in trouble. For many children, respecting their parents is a tough obligation. True enough, many parents hardly deserve the honor of their children. Likewise, many parents feel there are limits to the love they can give to their children, especially when, in their teens and during their adolescence, they dabble in things that God, and their parents, forbade. The sad reality is that so many families fall apart—resulting in children being estranged from their parents and vice versa, and brothers and sisters who have not even talked on the phone to each other for years. All too often funerals are the only occasions at which relatives and even family members briefly meet.

That is not to say that all familial happiness has ceased to exist. Fortunately, lots of children still adore their moms and dads, and are adamant that they have the best mommies and daddies in the world. Numerous adults continue to love their parents and care for them beyond the call of "normal" filial duty. Millions of thoroughly happy families do tons of things together and radiate the kind of solidarity and intimacy that are the envy of the neighborhood. And loads of brothers and sisters remain close throughout their entire life. So not all is lost, and there is still a lot of love going around.

What makes the difference? Again, it is the divine edge to this love. Love for parents, children, and relatives must model itself after the love of the Great Parent for His children and after the love of the Great Brother, who became love personified when He walked among us. It is primarily this gift love that makes the difference—the love that gives and forgives; the love that first looks after the interests of the other; the love that knows of true sacrifice. To the extent that these Christian values are incorporated into our family life, to that extent happiness comes within our reach. Many non-Christians, wittingly or unwittingly, operate by "Christian" rules and hugely benefit from it. Many Christians do so as well. Quite a few Christians, on the other hand, would be a lot more successful in the management of their family relationships if they would truly practice the principles of Christian love and ensure that their love has a divine edge to it.

Respect your parents! Love your children! Treat your relatives as you would like them to treat you. It can be something that becomes almost natural. On the other hand, particular circumstances can make it a tall order. But if we let God's love inform our love and ask Him to help us to love in a similar unselfish fashion as He does, it will work wonders.

3. Loving your friends. Often it is easier to love friends than family. After all, you can select your friends, but you usually have very little influence, if any at all, about those who are or become your parents, brothers, or sisters. There exists, however, quite a bit of difference between so-called friends and true friends. When people boast "I have lots of friends," most often they simply tell you that they have a few acquaintances whose last names they may, or may not know. Genuine friendship requires a major investment of oneself. To many, friendship is no more than networking. One needs "friends," especially in the right (high) places. But they are not the kind that one may love more than a brother (Prov. 18:24).

It is important to have friends. We live in all kinds of social networks that are mostly functional. Usually we have superiors, and many of us deal with people who report to us. Hopefully, we get on well with most of them, but they are not necessarily our friends. Friends provide an immensely valuable dimension to life. Friends talk. Friends listen. Friends give support. They have time for us, and if they do not have time, they will make it. They laugh with us. Or they cry with us. They encourage us or tell us we goofed terribly. Christian friends also pray for us and with us. They sometimes disappoint us. But true friendship can survive this.

God's love for us has a sublime friendship quality. On behalf of His Father, Christ said to His followers: "Now you are my friends" (John 15:15). Such friendship implies infinitely more than sharing our e-mail address or cell phone number. It involves identification of interests and aspirations. True friendship with the divine edge is gift love in *optima forma*.

4. *Love for animals.* All animals, great and small, "bright and beautiful," have one thing in common: "the Lord God made them all." So James Herriot told us. He was spot-on. Animals are more than commodities to be exploited at our convenience and for our pleasure. As custodians of God's creation we have a special duty with respect to animal care and welfare. People around the world have domesticated different species of animals for work and for pleasure. That is fine, as long as we treat such animals humanely. Many people not only *have* animals, but *love* animals. There is nothing wrong with this, provided they do not treat them on a par with human beings. "Love" for a cat, a dog, or some other pet can lead to emotional attachments that are unhealthy. Before we judge too harshly, we must realize that it is a sad comment on our society that some people have no other contact with living beings than with their pet, and are so lonely that they love their pet simply because they have no other human being around that appreciates their love.

Does God's love for us have anything to do with our respect and care for animals? Only in a certain sense. Love is relational, and there cannot be a relationship between a human being and a pet that compares with that between God and us. Yet even our "love" for animals can have a divine edge. When we realize that we are custodians and stewards of God's creation, it will give a new dimension to our loving care for animals. This extends beyond animal life to other things "bright and beautiful" in nature to (in the words of Ellen White) "every spire of springing grass" that has the words "God is love" written upon it.

5. *Love for things.* Even our "love" for things can be shaped by God's love for us. Love for things—material as well as immaterial—can easily deteriorate into greed and selfishness. Things (objects or projects) can easily become idols. Even great ideals can be pressed

into the service of our own inflated egos. Love for money remains the greatest threat to our spiritual well-being. It is, according to the apostle Paul, "at the root of all kinds of evil" (1 Tim. 6:10). Love for our car, our house, our garden, our hobby, and our membership in the local Lions Club are not wrong per se. In fact, all such things can enhance our happiness. But only as long as there remains a divine edge even to this kind of "love," and as long as we do not relentlessly focus on *getting* (let alone *taking*), but always make *giving* part of the equation.

6. *Love for the church.* We will touch upon our love for the church in a later chapter. If ever there should be a divine edge to our love, it is with respect to our relationship to God's community of believers. Gift love, rather than get love, defines the privileges and responsibilities of church membership.

Love with everything we are and have

"All you need is love." It sounds easy. In a way it is easy, for what could be a more natural response to our rich blessings than spontaneous love. But there is more to it. To love can be hard work. It can be intense, involving everything that we are and have—our heart (our emotions), our mind (our intellect), and our soul (or being). Loving requires our willingness to press all our talents and skills into the service of Christ. And we can be sure that at some point it will demand sacrifice.

Deepening our Christian experience is not a matter of learning to work harder, or of becoming smarter when we argue about biblical topics, but rather of learning to love more fully. It is a matter of replacing take love and get love with gift love, and thus exhibiting the kind of love that "comes from God" (1 John 4:7). Paul prayed for the Christians in Thessalonica: "May the Lord bring you into an ever deeper understanding of the love of God" (2 Thess. 3:5). That is also what we constantly must be praying for: an ever-deeper understanding of God's marvelous "gift love."

FAITH   2

"True, saving faith is a precious treasure of inestimable value. It is not superficial. The just lives by faith a truly spiritual, Christlike life. It is through faith that the steps are taken one at a time up the ladder of progress. Faith must be cultivated. It unites the human with the divine nature."

—ELLEN G. WHITE, *Our High Calling,* p. 67

"Faith" is a word with different shades of meaning. We speak, for instance, of the Christian faith or, more specifically, of the Catholic faith, the Baptist faith, or the Adventist faith, etc. When used in that sense, it refers to a set of doctrines, a series of beliefs. Those who adhere to the Christian faith are either members of a Christian church or regard themselves as belonging, to a greater or lesser extent, to the Christian tradition. The word can also be employed in its plural form: there exit a multitude of different faiths—i.e., faith communities and religious systems.

This chapter will not primarily use the word "faith" as a term that helps to classify people according to their religious convictions, but in its deeper meaning, in which we can employ it only in the singular. We will be thinking about faith as something within us— as trust. Admittedly, we will find that it is not so easy to provide a final, fully satisfying definition. Trust can have different gradations. We can trust in things or in the weather. I have faith in the bridge that I cross and in the engine of my car. I watch the news on television and can choose to trust the weather forecast (at least to some extent.) I can trust myself and my own abilities (whether it is wise to do so is another matter). I can place trust in my friends and in my colleagues, in my children and in my spouse. It is not difficult to see that trusting my son or my daughter operates at a different level than having trust in the reliability of the train timetable. When I trust a person, the aspect of *relationship* enters the picture.

Faith in God is relational trust at the highest level. It is not primarily believing some truths *about* God; it is believing *in* God (who is absolutely trustworthy) and entering into an intimate relationship with Him. The word "faith" and its related form "faithful" appear more than 300 times in the Bible. The author of the letter to the Hebrews provides, however, the only instance in which Scripture attempts a definition. Faith, according to this description, is "the confident assurance that what we hope for is going to happen. It is the evidence of things we cannot yet see" (Heb. 11:1).

So faith in the full biblical meaning is an inner certainty on which one can base an intimate relationship. It is more that having confidence in a book, even if that book is called the Bible. And it is more than having confidence in a church, even if that church is named Seventh-day Adventist. Saving faith—the kind of faith that truly counts—is trusting in the living God of the universe and in His faithful care for me. The faith that sets the believers apart at the end of time as the remnant people is not faith in a long list of doctrines, however important they may be, but faith in a *person*. They express their loyalty and trust in God through the keeping of God's commandments and *the faith of Jesus* (Rev. 14:12; 19:10).

Faith as a gift

Having faith seems quite natural, for we have faith in all kinds of things, and, unless we are extremely suspicious and distrustful, we place our trust in—at least some—other people. Few of us would ever go to the doctor if we did not at least have some trust in his or her knowledge and experience. We would not go to dentists if we did not have at least some faith in their ability to find out what might be wrong with our teeth, and then to do something about it. And we would not put a letter in the mailbox if we did not have a reasonable degree of faith in the postal services, however much that faith has at times been put to the test.

But when it comes to the most important relationship that one can imagine—faith in God—many will say that they simply do not have that faith and also have no idea what they would need to do to *get* that faith. "Get" is actually the right word. For faith is not the result of a lot of hard work, of late reading or concentrated thinking. Rather, faith is a free gift, for which we cannot take any credit ourselves (Eph. 2:8). That does not mean that reading and thinking (and praying, in particular) have no place in the process of receiving the gift of faith. Faith, Paul says, comes from listening to the message of good news (Rom. 10:17). So placing yourself in a situation where you can hear God's Word—when you listen to a friend, read the Bible, visit a church, or open yourself up to God in nature—will at least make it more likely that the gift comes your way.

Some appear to resist the gift of faith or want to have it only on their own terms—that is, with no strings attached.

Faith has a childlike quality (Ps. 116:6; Luke 10:21). Children do not negotiate when a free gift is within reach. They simply rush forward to grasp it with both hands. Being open to the gift is essential. But hanging on to it is also crucial. For you can lose your faith, as has happened to a major portion of yesterday's and today's generation in the secular Western world. The childlike longing for the gift seems to have been replaced, on a large scale, by a blatant disregard for something simple, and by a superficial desire for things that are more fashionable. There may, however, also be good news. In particular among the postmodern young generation, the inner openness for religion is coming back and faith is, once again, on the wish list.

Faith and evidence

The definition in the eleventh chapter of the letter to the Hebrews refers to *evidence*. But note that the text does not state that we have lots of hard evidence that we can draw on to corroborate our faith. It affirms that faith itself is evidence of some kind. It indicates that things that are as yet unseen—the things that are in another realm; things that are spiritual—are discerned in a spiritual way (1 Cor. 2:14).

Yet the question keeps coming back: How much evidence is there for our faith? Is there a "firm foundation" on which we can confidently build? Yes, but however strong this "firmness" may appear, it is not absolute. One might ask: Is the Bible not unshakable evidence for our faith in God? Do we not have the prophetic word that is utterly sure? (2 Peter 1:19). Does the "spade" not "confirm the book"? Are the results of biblical archaeology not sufficient to sway even the most sceptical person? And do the great classical arguments for the existence of God not continue to provide a formidable foundation of logic that remains as valid as ever? Or has every truth become utterly relative in today's postmodern climate?

All these lines of reasoning still have their value. But in the last resort they do not offer absolute and unshakable evidence. Our prophetic studies provide great insights, but they frequently also leave us with unresolved questions. Not all findings of biblical archaeology fit neatly into the chronology we have established, and at times we have no choice but to suspend judgment and allow mysteries to remain. Also, the great proofs for the existence of God may still convince people that logic demands that there is a god, but they do not automatically lead them to the personal God of Abraham, Isaac, and Jacob, the God whom we know as the Father of our Lord Jesus Christ.

Let us face it: What hard evidence can there be for the true value of an intimate human relationship? Likewise, when we try to understand the things that belong to the realm of the divine, all comparisons will, at best, only partially apply. Consider for a moment the relationship between a wife and her husband. Let us assume that we are dealing with a solid and satisfying marriage. But what indisputable evidence do these two people have that their relation is, in fact, real and that it is, in actual fact, a love relationship?

I am writing these lines in a guest room at a college where I happen to be lecturing for a few weeks. My wife has stayed home. We remain in daily contact by e-mail and telephone. While I have no doubt that my wife loves me and does not cheat on me, what hard evidence do I have? She could be meeting a secret lover at this very moment, without any risk of me finding out. When I come home, and she tells me she has missed me, she may just pretend in a quite convincing way. She may kiss me while her thoughts are with someone else, whom she finds more attractive and more fun to be with. However, I disregard all these possibilities. I believe, I have enough evidence to think that, for some reason, she continues to love me. We have a relationship that needs no further total verification. In fact, if I were looking for some kind of absolute evidence, I would seriously harm the relationship. For example, I could hire a private detective to check up on my wife while I am gone. The report of the detective may be totally reassuring, but I would not want to share it with her. The very existence of that piece of evidence would gravely damage the relationship of trust between us.

Granted, the comparison is imperfect. But it does make an important point. My relationship with my wife does not need the evidence provided by a private eye. I know from experience, and I need no further hard evidence that love between human beings is something real and wonderful. Faith in God does not need absolute evidence either. The faith relationship between God and us *is* evidence of the divine love that ever continues to reach out to us!

Faith and reason

Many books have titles combining the words "faith" and "reason," and countless conferences and seminars explore the relationship between those two concepts. They are part of the centuries-old ever-ongoing discussion as to what extent we can harmonize the traditional Christian faith content with the findings of "modern" science. Some will argue that this is a fruitless enterprise. Faith, they say, does not function on the same plane as science, and they each deal with their own kind of truth. Many Christians have even been suspicious of intellectual endeavors, and of the results of modern science. Tending to separate faith from science, they have said: If what you believe conflicts with what you learn from science, you choose your faith and abandon your science!

Others will vehemently disagree. They will maintain that faith (*theology* might, in this context, be a better term) and science study one and the same reality. They may have different methods, and may work from different premises, but ultimately they each try to discover more about one and the same truth. This is the position most

Adventist scholars hold, even though in the course of time, many have come to the insight that our human knowledge is so fragmentary, that we must expect to find ourselves left with many unanswered questions and thus must not too quickly be alarmed if our current scientific findings do not seem to match seamlessly with all of our theological positions. But, whatever difficulties remain or paradigm shifts may yet be needed, the study of our world and of the universe is not detached from our faith. The heavens (and the subatomic particles and everything in between) in marvelous ways, "tell of the glory of God" and "the skies display his marvelous craftsmanship" (Ps. 19:1).

The question of the relationship between faith and reason has a possibly even more important aspect. How rational is our faith? To what extent does our relationship with God depend on our ability to *understand* who and what God is? Is having faith compatible with reason, or is faith irrational and mainly a matter of emotion, feeling, intuition, a sixth sense, or something in that sphere?

Christians must, by definition, be thinking persons. Scripture tells them to love God also with their *mind* (Matt. 22:37). Not all Christians live up to this. The famous philosopher Bertrand Russell reportedly once remarked: "Most Christians would rather die than think. In fact, they do."[1] This has been especially true in evangelical circles. Maybe the title of a book that created quite a bit of a stir best sums up the issue: *The Scandal of the Evangelical Mind*, by Mark Knoll.[2] Many evangelical Christians have argued that too much knowledge is dangerous. Did not Paul say that knowledge only "makes us feel important" (see 1 Cor. 8:1, 2), that it tends to lead to arrogance and loss of faith? The apostle certainly did not, however, propose that all thinking is negative and ill-advised. He did not oppose *good* thinking, but *inaccurate* thinking. Paul wanted us to be intentional in our thinking. "Fix your thoughts on what is true and honorable and right," he said (Phil. 4:8). And, whatever you do, do it to the glory of God. So use your mind to His glory.

This is not to say, however, that human thought is the answer to everything. Here we are back to the question of our "firm foundation." It is a topic that we cannot adequately deal with in a short chapter such as this. But let me briefly state what my conviction is, and then, I suggest, you take some time to think carefully about it. Human beings are rational beings. When the famous Descartes (1596-1650) launched his dictum "I think, therefore I am," the era of the Enlightenment, which elevated human rationality to the supreme position it would hold until quite recently, began. Before Descartes, reason already had an important place. The great medieval theologian Anselm had said, "I believe so that I may understand." But now the equation shifted, and the Cartesian philosophy, in fact, proposed that we ought to rephrase his statement into: "I believe only what I can understand."

The Christian religion in its various forms became a highly rationalistic enterprise. It was true for Protestantism in particular—Adventism very definitely included. Adventists *studied* (rather than *read*) the Bible to differentiate between the biblical Truth and the error of ecclesiastical tradition. They built a doctrinal system that, they felt, was cohesive and logical. As a result they defended their positions with fervor and were delighted that in religious debates their arguments usually won the day. God, they were convinced, had given them a brain, in order to study and continuously advance in a better understanding of the truth.

During the past few decades we have, however, seen a momentous shift in people's approach to religion. Many Christians—and again, many Adventist Christians included—have been deeply influenced by the so-called postmodern thinking. One of the key postmodern convictions is that knowledge does not only—or, some would say, even primarily—emerge from our ability to reason, but also from other, nonrational sources. Why should we trust our brains more than our senses? Why should we distrust our intuition and feelings? Postmodern people do not place all their eggs in the basket of reason, but also emphasize the value of experience. This new way of thinking has had an enormous influence on the approach of today's generation to religious truth.

In a number of ways it is a positive development. Many Christians—including Adventist Christians—have traditionally laid so much stress on thinking and on building doctrinal structures and arguing about their religion that nonrational aspects, such as awe and wonder, have tended to remain underdeveloped. The challenge we face is one of maintaining balance. Although our faith is more than ratio (reason), it is not irrational. When we welcome a greater role for the nonrational, reason does not go out of the window. The Christian message is a coherent story that is at least as intellectually defensible as any nontheistic worldview. But faith in God is immeasurably more than acquiring and further developing a series of religious views that can stand the rigor of academic examination. Faith is not detached from doctrinal content. Nor is it to be excised from the realm of thought. It is, however, in the first place a relationship of trust that brings an inner peace that is "far more wonderful than the human mind can understand" (Phil. 4:7).

Faith and community

One of the hot theological issues of our time is the relationship between faith and community. Many theologians influenced by postmodernity believe that the content of one's faith (here in the sense of one's doctrinal beliefs) is to a large degree determined by the community to which one belongs. Each community has its own traditions and speaks its own kind of theological language. Of course, we may learn from dialogue with others. To that extent we would have no quarrel with this approach. But it is impossible to agree with the postmodern notion that the content of our faith is largely *determined* by the community we happen to be part of, and that we are merely participating in a "language game" when we talk about our religious views, in our own jargon, within the context of our particular subculture. The community does not *create* a particular version of the truth. It is the other way round: the truth creates a particular kind of community. Naturally, the community of which we are part influences the way in which we continue to express the truth. But being part of our faith community loses most of its meaning if the faith that we subscribe to is nothing more than the subjective opinion of a group of people that is totally, or even mostly, conditioned by the traditions and customs of the group.

The community has an important role in the nurture of the faith, both in the sense that it can help its members to mature in their under-standing of the teachings that it has embraced, and in the sense of grow-ing in the intimacy of the faith relationship with God. This happens through its worship, its prayers, and its desire to gain greater depth in understanding of the Bible. The church at Berea, where Paul discovered an extraordinary open-mindedness, and where the members searched the Scriptures day after day, remains a shining example of a community where the faith of the believers could grow (Acts 17:10-12).

Faith and work

Throughout the centuries Christians have struggled to get the right balance between *faith* and *works*. On the one hand, many have made works the basis for their spiritual experience and have primar-ily trusted in their own efforts and sacrifices to get enough spiritual merits in order to make it into heaven eventually. Others have gone so far as to claim that outward practices have no influence on one's salvation. We are saved by faith only, they claim, while referring to Paul's statements in his letter to the Romans (Rom. 1:17).

Putting faith *over and against* works creates a false dilemma. Faith does not replace works. The law is not done away with because we have faith. It is only "when we have faith" that "we truly fulfill the law" (Rom. 3:31). It will become our second nature to live by the guidelines that God has provided in the laws that He gave to human beings as provisions to increase their happiness. God's law, if rightly understood, does not chain us up and restrict our movements. On the contrary, "the law . . . sets you free!" (James 1:25).

Neither is faith to be in *balance* with our efforts to do good and keep the law. Salvation is only through faith in Christ. It comes as the result of what Christ did, and not through what we do. Human effort will always be totally inadequate. Our relationship with the Lord rests on our faith in Him, and not upon any trust in what we ourselves might bring to the table.

Faith and doubt

Faith and doubt go together. I am very suspicious when people tell me that their relationship with God has always been constant, and that they have never doubted. Either they are not telling the full truth or they have never done much serious thinking. Most of us are very much like the man who came to Jesus with the request that He heal his son, who was possessed by an evil spirit. The statement he made to Jesus finds an echo in the desperate cry of countless people: "I do believe, but help me not to doubt" (Mark 9:24). The story of how the apostle Thomas doubted that Jesus had truly risen (John 20:24-29) has always been an encouragement for me. Just imagine: a disciple who had been for more than three years with Jesus could still doubt without being turned away by the Master.

Faith comes in different gradations. Time and again Jesus speaks of those who have but little faith (e.g., Matt. 6:30; 8:10). On the other hand, the Bible refers to those who have "great" or "mature" faith (Matt. 15:28; 1 John 2:13). It also mentions the possibility that faith is further "strengthened" (e.g., Acts 15:32; 16:5), and that believers "grow" in their faith (Phil. 1:25). Some interesting research indicates that the growth of faith tends to follow a particular pattern and there exist clearly recognizable stages in the maturation of faith during an individual's life span. Fascinating though that research may be, it is not important for our actual "walk of faith" to be able to analyze how God's gift of faith interacts with our mind and soul. What counts is that our trust deepens as we continue to journey with our Lord, and that our faith relationship reaches an ever-closer intimacy.

---

[1] This is attributed to Bertrand Russell, but the source is unknown.
[2] Grand Rapids: William B. Eerdmans Pub. Co., 1994.

HOPE   3

"I know not when my Lord may come,
At night or noonday fair,
Nor if I walk the vale with Him,
Or meet Him in the air.

"But 'I know whom I have believed,
And am persuaded that He is able
To keep that which I've committed
Unto Him against that day.'"

—The Seventh-day Adventist Hymnal, no. 511

Recently I taught a class as part of a master's degree program for future pastors. The course title was "Approaches to the Contemporary Mind." The students came from a number of vastly different cultures. Having taught this class a number of times, I am increasingly aware of how difficult it is to dialogue about "the contemporary mind" with a diverse group of students—a few from Western Europe and the United States, some from what was once called Eastern Europe (a region now more commonly referred to as Central Europe), and some from sub-Saharan Africa and from such countries as Pakistan and Egypt. In one of the class periods we addressed the outlook that people have regarding the future. One of the older students from Pakistan made an interesting observation. He told us that, when he lived in Pakistan, his children were adamant that they wanted to become doctors and professors. Now that they had been living in Britain for the past five years, he said, they were far less ambitious and just hoped that they would eventually finish school and find a job.

His comment illustrates the fundamental shift that has taken place in the Western world in the past few decades. I belong to a generation that was still very optimistic and ambitious about the future. Our parents were convinced that we, their children, would do much better than they had been able to do. We would get a better education than they had had the chance to obtain. And we would get better jobs and attain a much higher standard of living. In many cases our parents lived to see their expectations fulfilled. But the generation that I am part of now has children in their late 30s, and some have grandchildren who are getting ready to begin their secondary education. What do we see? The present younger generations in the West no longer believe that they will be able to reach higher than their parents. Some are not so sure that they even *want* to do "better," if this "better" also means, as they fear, an even more competitive and more stressful life. The post-World War II generation was going to build a new society—things could only improve. Those growing up and starting a career in the early twenty-first century very much doubt that they have inherited the kind of world that can bring future happiness. They view the political mess and the ecological threats around the world; they notice the superficial consumerism and the unstoppable retreat of traditional values, and they recognize how a major percentage of the earth's population—which keeps growing at an alarming rate—does not share in the affluence that so many others enjoy. And they know that the current reckless exploitation of the earth's resources is not sustainable.

There may not be the widespread kind of despair that existentialist philosophers like Jean-Paul Sartre wrote about, but certainly a pervasive concern and pessimism about the future lingers. And though many will still say that life is not too bad, a staggering number of people find their inner life characterized by meaninglessness and emptiness. Some of the countries that once were part of the old Soviet order now have the highest suicide statistics in the world. The wild hope that engulfed these countries when "the wall" came tumbling down has all too quickly dissipated, and has left a large part of the population frustrated and in many ways worse off than they were before.

What is hope?

People often use the word "hope" very loosely and superficially. A wide chasm lurks between the profound hope introduced to us in the Bible and the shallow, so-called hope of large numbers of people around us. Those who buy their weekly or monthly lottery ticket *hope* that this time they will hit the jackpot in a big way. Yet their hope is, in fact, no more than a gamble, and the likelihood that they will actually win a major prize is about the same as the chance of finding 10 $100 notes in a wastepaper bin in the office.

Hope in the biblical sense is not the same as being optimistic, such as *hoping* that a project that one has been working on will actually succeed. Whether the project will come to fruition will be mainly determined by the planning that went into it, and the skills of those who execute it. Even if the project is of a religious nature and people have invested a lot of prayer in addition to sweat, the hope that such a project will end well is not the same as the kind of hope we have regarding Christ's second coming. We must not confuse living in hope, in the full Christian sense of the word, with the easy possibility thinking of popular psychology or of the preachers of the health and wealth gospel that send their slick broadcasts around the globe. Hope that chemotherapy will stop the onslaught of cancer, however encouraging the statistics are, is not the same kind of thing as the Christian hope of eternal life.

Hope is closely tied to faith. The German theologian Jürgen Moltmann defines biblical hope as *believing hope.* "'Hope is nothing else,'" he writes, quoting John Calvin, "'than the expectation of those things which faith has believed to have been truly promised by God. Thus faith believes God to be true, hope awaits the time when this truth shall be manifested.'" Then he adds his own words, "Without faith's knowledge of Christ, hope becomes a utopia and remains hanging in the air. But without hope, faith falls to pieces. . . . It is through faith that man finds the path of true life, but it is only hope that keeps him on that path. Thus it is that faith in Christ gives hope its assurance. Thus it is that hope gives faith in Christ its breadth and leads it into life."[1]

The Hope of the Second Coming

The hope of the Adventist Christian culminates in the expectation of Christ's return to this earth, when the individual believer gets his or her eternal lease on real life, and when God cleanses the earth of sin and the 1,000-year process of full restoration to divine perfection gets under way. "We look forward to that wonderful event when the glory of our great God and Savior, Jesus Christ, will be revealed" (Titus 2:13). Nothing else can give that ultimate assurance that the problems of humanity will at last be solved. Who can really believe that the politicians are going to sort things out in any final way? And even if they were able to arrange for world peace, how would they undo the ecological damage to our globe? Is there any reason to think that science would solve all of our troubles? Yes, science may extend our average life span 10 or 12 years, but we would still continue to stare mortality in its lifeless face.

It is true that 20 centuries have passed since Christ made His solemn promise: "When everything is ready, I will come and get you, so that you will always be with me, where I am" (John 14:3). It seems that the apostles expected this to take place within years. Paul talks of "we who are still alive" (1 Thess. 4:17) at the moment of Christ's coming, clearly indicating that there would at least be a good possibility that Jesus would return during his own life time. Ever since, Christians have taken Jesus' promise "Yes, I am coming soon!" (Rev. 22:20) at face value, and have interpreted "soon" in a very human way. Often they have not been able to resist the temptation to calculate specific dates. Just as often they have been bitterly disappointed and have realized too late that such calculations are futile, since no one will ever know beforehand when the final hour strikes. Christ Himself made it very clear: "No one knows the day or the hour when these things will happen, not even the angels in heaven or the Son himself. Only the Father knows" (Matt. 24:36).

Seventh-day Adventists have preached the message of Christ's soon return with fervor for approximately 150 years. Gradually more and more church leaders and "ordinary" church members are beginning to wonder—and to voice their concern—about how we can retain the urgency of our message after such a long period of time. Adventist authors have written quite a few books that deal with this "apparent" delay. Even though Christ warned us not to be like the servant who neglected his duties, thinking, 'My master won't be back for a while' (Matt. 24:48), we still struggle with the temptation to join the "scoffers" in their argument: "Jesus promised to come back, did he? Then where is he? Why, as far back as anyone can remember everything has remained exactly the same since the world was first created" (2 Peter 3:4).

Surely our patience is tested. And for a good reason. God is "patient for your sake," Peter writes to the first-century Christians, as well as to us. God's love is the key to understanding the apparent delay. "He does not want anyone to perish, so he is giving more time for everyone to repent" (verse 9). The disciple reminds us of our common mistake to think too much in human terms when arguing about God's dealings with us. The fact that we live such short lives conditions our concept of time. For us "soon" must mean within a few years. For our eternal God, however, time is a very different commodity. "You must not forget, dear friends," Peter explains, "that a day is like a thousand years to the Lord, and a thousand years is like a day" (verse 8).

Adventist Christians must not lose their hope. Many of us may, however, have to learn to be even more patient. That is not so easy. After all, are we not living in the last days, in the end of time? And do the "signs of the times" not tell us that Christ's coming is "very near, right at the door" (Matt. 24:33)? Yes indeed, but at the same time there is a broader picture. Adventist theologian Jon Paulien had done us a tremendous service by putting end-time thinking in a clearer biblical perspective than many of us have so far seen.[2] He explains that in a sense God's people have always been living with "the end" of time in mind. They have always faced the constant tension between *what is* and *what is to come*. This is not to say that history has no movement. We are inevitably drawing closer to the grand finale. But we still "do not know the day or hour" of His return (Matt. 25:13).

How do we react?

The Bible provides us with numerous "signs" of the "soon" return of Christ. What are they? Are they specific points along a predetermined time path that leads us to the ushering in of the kingdom? The New Testament word for this type of "sign" is *semeion*. It may refer to a miraculous event, but not necessarily so. Its basic meaning is that of a mark, a token, or an omen that announces coming events.[3]

The word "signal" may be the best translation. Ever since Christ announced His return, signals along the way have pointed us to that great event. Signals alerted the first-century church that Christ's promises were certain. The medieval Christians were also able to discern clear signals that history was moving toward its culmination. The Adventist pioneers were convinced that such signals as the famous Lisbon earthquake of 1755 and the Dark Day of May 19, 1780, were astounding indications that time was running out. Natural disasters of all kinds, political unrest, ecological threats, international terrorism, and widespread moral degradation are just as powerful signals in our days that Christ's coming is still very much part of the divine agenda.

Such signals ought to give ample reason for joyful anticipation.. Remember the words of the Lord: "When all these things begin to happen, stand straight and look up, for your salvation is near!" (Luke 21:28). Unfortunately, that is not how all Adventists experience the Christian hope. Fear taints the hope of many, and deep anxiety destroys their joy. As Adventists we read, talk, and preach about the developments and events that will precede the day of Christ's return, and it often creates great concern in our hearts. Revelation 16, with its prediction of the last plagues, for example, does not exactly encourage most of us. Even though it tells us that the seven last plagues target the unbelievers, the chapter does not leave us with the impression that the period just prior to Christ's second coming is something to look forward to. *Who will be able to survive when this time arrives?* (Rev. 6:17). We wonder. We have developed our own peculiar Adventist jargon when we speak of the future that awaits humanity: a time of trouble, the passage of Sunday laws, a time of persecution, a "death decree" for those who do not have the "mark of the beast," the close of probation, etc.

For many Advent believers fear is the overwhelming emotion when they think about the end of time. Will they make it when it really gets rough? How will it be when the door of grace has shut and they will have to survive without a Mediator? How perfect must they be? And will they ever reach that state of absolute perfection? Many worry that they might not reach that point. Some, on the other hand, believe they have achieved it already, or are very close. Often such individuals are not the most pleasant persons to deal with, and usually it does not require the spiritual gift of discernment to perceive that they have not, in any case, overcome the sin of pride. One might well ask: How can a religion based on faith, hope, and love result in so much fear? How does that agree with the words of the apostle John that "perfect love expels all fear" (1 John 4:18)?

Living in hope

How do we deal with this thorny issue? Increasingly our church profiles itself as a community of hope. We refer to what we preach as a message of hope. And we have launched a worldwide television channel that we have named the Hope Channel. I am happy with that positive emphasis. After all, this is biblical language. All of us should be looking forward to a "wonderful event" (Titus 2:13). Always we should be pleased to talk about it and explain what it entails (1 Peter 3:15). It should make people happy when we share our Advent message. Why then does it make so many scared and uncertain?

The solution to the dilemma cannot be that we trivialize or simply ignore the end-time scenario. We would be totally wrong if we take away the utter seriousness of living "in the last days." The parable of the 10 bridesmaids who went to meet their bridegroom (Matt. 25: 1-13) makes it clear that the expectation of Christ's soon arrival presupposes constant alertness and thorough preparation. The story ends with Christ's urgent warning: "Stay awake and be prepared, because you do not know the day or hour of my return" (verse 13). Staying awake and making of preparations should, however, not take the form of blind obsession. Taking careful note of the signals along the way toward God's future should not encourage us to entertain wild speculations and develop bizarre conspiracy theories—let alone push them on others as special truths. The Bible calls for balance. "Keep alert and pray" (Matt. 26:41). And: "Occupy till I come" (Luke 19:13, KJV).

We find such balance uniquely expressed in Luke 21, the chapter about the signs of the coming kingdom that runs parallel to the more well-known version of Matthew 24. Yes, Jesus warns us, it will not be easy, for "there will be a time of great persecution" (verse 12). But do not forget that God is with you, and thus "don't worry about how to answer the charges against you" (verse 14). Yes, even those who are closest to you may betray you (verses 16, 17). Yet "not a hair of your head will perish! By standing firm, you will win your souls" (verses 18, 19). Again, "there will be strange events" and "the courage of many people will falter" (verses 25, 26). Yet be of good courage, for "your salvation is near" (verse 28).

Underneath the sense of unqualified seriousness and the awareness that things will be heating up to a level that we cannot yet imagine, there is a fundamental attitude of hope. Beneath all questions and doubt that might raise their ugly head, there is the indestructible certainty that all will be well. "We have this hope that burns within our hearts, hope in the coming of the Lord."[4]

A message of hope

What this world (including the church and each one of us individually) needs is a message of hope. The mission of the church is to communicate hope: true, pure, unlimited hope. The message of the secularists who preach a message of political and socioeconomic hope will not do. Nor will the evolutionary worldview do either. Even if this theory were true (which we know it is not), who would want to wait another 100 million years or so before our planet has outgrown its present inadequacies? What kind of hope would that be? The message of liberal Christianity, with its moral (unfounded) optimism, will not do. American theologian H. Richard Niebuhr once described its message as a witness of "a God without wrath, [who] brought men without sin into a kingdom without judgment through the ministrations of a Christ without a cross."[5] Such a message is, indeed, totally devoid of genuine hope and will not do. But let us also be very critical of the message of hope that often emerges from fundamentalist quarters, with its one-sided emphasis on hell and damnation that so often tends to eclipse the promise of restoration. And with its unbiblical views of a rapture and other expectations that confuse rather than inspire. In addition, let us refuse to listen to the bizarre theories of conspiracy-adepts who see a scheming Jesuit behind every tree and a vast network of secret societies that stretches its tentacles into every church and political organisation.

The message of hope that we must preach and that gives structure to our faith is one of unflinching certainty. The future of both our planet and the church is safe. My own personal destiny is secure. Humanity's problems will find their ultimate solution. The church will weather all the storms of the present and the future. My present existence is a mere introduction to the endless future that God has provided for me above and beyond death. We are privileged to have this deep-rooted certainty that does not depend primarily on intellectual convictions. Our hope that Christ's coming is approaching does not rest on a constant counting and recounting of famines, wars, and earthquakes, however important such signals are. Nor does it derive from intricate schedules of last-day events that can tell us where exactly we are on the prophetic time path—though a close reading of the prophetic portions of the Bible is still important.

Ultimately our hope is based on a Person and His promises. Christ is our hope. He is the truth. His words will not fail. Because of our faith relationship with Him, we can build on what He has said. We do not trust just on the basis of events that fall into place in the way we expected them to happen. We trust in a Person, who has never let us down. He says: I will come back. I will sort this world out. *My* resurrection is the guarantee of *your* resurrection. And faith in Me will get you through, regardless of the challenges that may lie ahead of you. My kingdom is already among you (see Luke 17:21), but will soon become glorious reality in its final glory.

This certainty takes care of all our fears. With Paul we can say: "I know the one in whom I trust, and I am sure that he is able to guard what I have entrusted to him until the day of his return" (2 Tim. 1:12).

---

[1] Jürgen Moltmann, *Theology of Hope* (London: SCM Press, Ltd., 1967), p. 20.

[2] See Jon Paulien, *What the Bible Says About the End-time* (Hagerstown, Md.: Review and Herald Pub. Assn., 1994).

[3] Colin Brown, ed., *Dictionary of New Testament Theology* (Exeter: Paternoster Press, 1976), vol. 2, pp. 626ff.

[4] *The Seventh-day Adventist Hymnal* (Hagerstown, Md.: Review and Herald Pub. Assn., 1985) no. 214.

[5] H. Richard Niebuhr, *The Kingdom of God in America* (New York: Harper and Row, 1959), p. 193.

LIFE 4

"It is not a conclusive evidence that a man is a Christian because he manifests spiritual ecstasy under extraordinary circumstances. Holiness is not rapture: it is an entire surrender of the will to God; it is living by every word that proceeds from the mouth of God; it is doing the will of our heavenly Father; it is trusting God in trial, in darkness as well as in the light; it is walking by faith and not by sight; it is relying on God with unquestioning confidence, and resting in His love."

—ELLEN G. WHITE, *The Acts of the Apostles*, p. 51

Human beings have a universal interest in a good life. But opinions vary dramatically as to what a good life might be. According to one dictionary that I consulted a "good life" is a life situation characterized by a high standard of living. On one particular chat site someone responded to the question of what a good life is with the following remark: "The good life is in my opinion when you wake up every morning with no bills, no health problems, no drama, and no problems to worry about. When you go to sleep at night, you have the sense of a clear head and a comfortable carefree future." When, some time ago, a publisher launched a new glossy magazine for the Dutch market, it gave the periodical the title *Living*. The magazine described its mission as a lifestyle journal about the good things of life, with lots of interviews and articles about travel, beautiful homes, beauty and fashion, entertainment, eating, drinking, and partying.

The idea of a good life—also often referred to as a "full" life— is also present in the Bible. But there the emphasis is quite different. Christ told His followers that He had come to give them "life in all its fullness" (John 10:10), or, as other translations render it: a life "to the full" (NIV) or a way of living "more abundantly" (KJV). Such abundant life is, as we shall see, not adverse to many of the material and concrete enjoyments of the present life, but reaches far beyond it and offers dimensions totally unknown to the large masses that seek for a full life exclusively of what our affluent, secular society has on offer.

Physical life

In whatever way we define this full and abundant life, we will always, first of all, encounter a physical aspect. Living beings (God, angels, human beings, animals) or living things (plants) are alive. They differ in a fundamental way from nonliving things, however complex in structure the latter may be. What makes the difference? What precisely is the mysterious something that we call life? What is the crucial difference between a corpse and a living body, between an animal and an inanimate object, between a sophisticated robot and a human being?

We often speak of the *mystery* of life. Many feel this mystery will forever remain unsolved. Of course, many others believe that science will one day, sooner or later, unravel it. In many laboratories around the world scientists are trying to create life. The search has been on for a long time and is infinitely more sophisticated than the medieval idea that simple human interventions could create life. Today no one any longer assumes that by strategically placing some bits of cheese in a secluded place one could create life in the form of mice. Every once in a while we now hear that scientists are close to creating a "simple" virus, and as I write this chapter news items are appearing, claiming that for the first time researchers have produced a "synthetic virus." From what I understand of the reports, the American scientist who was responsible for this alleged breakthrough did not actually create anything, but succeeded in transplanting a so-called genome from one bacterium cell to another.

I have no idea what human brains will yet be able to discover or invent. But to claim that human science is on the brink of creating real life from "dead" material seems overly optimistic, to say the very least. The idea that life could, with or without a bit of human assistance, evolve from nonlife is, as we know, the basic presupposition of the evolutionary hypothesis. But nothing really sustains such a belief. Robert Shapiro, a professor emeritus of chemistry and senior research scientist at New York University and the author or coauthor of more than 125 publications primarily in the area of DNA chemistry, wrote: "The improbability involved in generating even one bacterium is so large that it reduces all considerations of time and space to nothingness. Given such odds, the time until the black holes evaporate and the space to the ends of the universe would make no difference at all. If we were to wait, we would truly be waiting for a miracle."[1] Sir Fred Hoyle, a famous British astronomer who rejected the evolutionary theories about the origin of the universe, compared the probability of life arising by chance to lining up 10^{50} (1 followed by 50 zeros) blind people, giving each one a scrambled Rubik's Cube, and finding that they all solve the cube at the same moment.[2]

Invariably, discussions about the "making" of life point out that we are looking for *simple* forms of life. The thought that any form of "simple" life exists is, however, seriously misleading. Experts tell us that one "simple" yeast cell has as many different components as a Boeing-777 airplane.

Thus far, creating life in a laboratory, synthetic or otherwise, seems to be as far removed from reality as were the many ancient and medieval myths about the fountain of youth. Even the search for an extension of our present life has not offered the kind of success that many hoped for and believed in. Humanity's mortality continues to stare it blatantly in the face. According to the Bible the earliest generations of humanity lived for centuries. Adam died at age 930, and Methuselah holds the all-time record of 969. As earth's history continued and the human race rapidly degenerated, such figures soon dropped dramatically. Today life expectancy rates in developed countries vary between 77 and 83 years, while some developing countries barely reach the 40-year mark. Individuals, of course, may well surpass the average age limit. The number of people reaching their hundredth birthday is on the increase. But such cases of longevity remain the exception rather than the rule. Reasonably reliable documentation can point to only about 20 people who have reached the age of 115. The record holder in modern times is Jeanne Calment, a French woman who died August 4, 1997, at age of 122 years and 164 days. She is the only person in modern history who indisputably lived for more than 120 years.

Individually, many people do whatever they can to postpone the aging process. Anti-aging foods, anti-aging medicines, and anti-aging food supplements have become big business. People routinely enlist anti-aging cosmetic products and extreme or less-extreme makeovers, with or without surgery, in the frantic fight against the onslaught of old age. Some of this may deliver some results, and better health care and an emphasis on a more responsible lifestyle are certainly useful. Therefore, in all probability life expectancy rates in the Western world will indeed continue to be on the increase. But experts are speaking in terms of a limited number of years and do not suggest that someday soon people will live 150 or 200 years or more! Life, both its beginning and its extension, retains its mysterious character. What applies to human life, is also true for other forms of life. A bristlecone pine tree in the White Mountains of California is reportedly the oldest known living tree on earth. It has stood there for some 4,700 years. A giant tortoise that died in 2006 in an Indian zoo was, it would appear, born around 1750. These forms of life certainly exceed even the life span of Jeanne Calment, but they do not provide a bridge to the origin of life in whatever form.

The living God—the source of life

Christians confidently declare that life is not a commodity that creatures can make or manipulate at will, and that all careful thinking about its origin will lead us to the realm of the Creator. God is the sole Source of life. Scripture defines the omnipotent God of the Bible as the *living* God and contrasts Him with the imaginary deities of the surrounding cultures (Ps. 42:2; 84:2). Simon Peter testified that Christ was no one else but the Son "of the living God." Christ uses a number of striking metaphors to underline that He, as the Son of the living God, can justifiably claim that life had its source in Him. In Him, Ellen White declared, is life—"original, unborrowed, underived."[3] God is the ultimate source of all physical life, whether human or nonhuman. In the Word was life itself. He created everything; there was nothing that He did not make (see John 1:4). This extends beyond the physical dimension of life. Christ, the Word, is the water of life (John 4:14), as well of the bread of life that sustains all human life worth living. Yes, He said, "I am the bread of life! . . . Who eats this bread will live forever" (John 6:48-51). He provides the only kind of life-sustaining nurture that enables us to enjoy life in its true sense, now and forevermore.

For centuries the Christian church has allowed itself to be influenced by pagan thought and has pictured the life that comes from God as something quite distinct from the body. It equated life with a nonmaterial something that it referred to as the *soul*. Theologians considered the soul to be immortal and as something that somehow could be separated from the body. At death the immortal soul would go to either heaven or hell. The pagan concept of a division of life into body and soul is, however, completely alien to the teachings of the Bible. More and more Christians today are now slowly accepting what Adventists have maintained from the beginning of their corporate existence, namely that the biblical view of humanity is holistic. Body and soul inseparably belong together. When God gives life, humans become living beings. But when death arrives, life is surrendered, but not as an immortal something that lives on in a spiritlike existence. As people die, they cease to be until the moment that the Lord will call them back to life.

Though God is the source of all life, and everything, including viruses, plants, animals, and humans, owes its existence to Him, human life is distinct from other forms of life on earth. The Lord has endowed human beings with personhood. Men and women can respond to their Creator and can make moral decisions. But make no mistake—it does not mean that human life is in essence a part of God and is therefore, in actual fact, divine. Though humanity's physical, emotional, and intellectual life stems from God, human beings are still creatures, and their life remains at all times a gift. While eternal life is an unearned gift, but our present life is just as much a gift from God.

That fact that life is a divine gift implies that we, as human beings, must realize both the depth of this truth and understand its far-reaching implications. This fundamental fact runs counter to the human-centered thinking that is so commonplace—particularly that we can manipulate life both at its beginning and toward its end. Yes, we have discovered much about the mechanics of fertility, cross-breeding, DNA, fetal development, the birthing process, etc. We have developed techniques to hasten or to postpone death. As a result we discuss the moral issues of abortion, fertility treatments, cloning, euthanasia, and the death penalty. Thus we weigh the interests of unborn children against those of the prospective mother. Should we urge a woman to carry to full term a child expected to have severe disabilities? In addition, we struggle with questions about war and peace and justice. And we find ourselves confronted with many decisions that previous generations did not have to face. Many of today's situations were unknown in Bible times. When Christians seek guidance in the Bible, they often are dismayed not to find clear-cut answers. Instead, they must search out the basic principles and then apply them prayerfully and conscientiously to the specific situations they encounter. For that reason no other Christian individual and no church organization can dictate what is right or wrong in every particular instance. However, there will always be at least a degree of subjectivity in the personal choice that remains our individual responsibility. And because of that, we must respect others if they come to a conclusion that we would not have arrived at ourselves.

Nonhuman life is just as much a domain of responsible human stewardship. Every creature owes its life to the Creator, and nonhuman life never becomes a simple commodity that we can treat or dispose of without any moral implications.

The value of life

This leads us to the next question. Even when we fully realize that life is a gift, we cannot escape the question as to the gift's value. Everything in this world has a price, whether it is our house, our car, a book, or a wedding. And whether we like it or not, in our day and age we tend to express the value of things—material and immaterial—in economic terms. So people constantly ask: What is the value of a human life? If someone begins a large building project, safety regulations play an increasingly important role, but society usually takes it for granted that some may die from construction accidents. How many lives are acceptable? When the authorities contemplate speeding limits and other traffic regulations, the government debates: What will it cost? Are the number of lives that may be saved worth these extra costs? How does the investment in research and development of new medicines relate to the number of cases that may be treated, and will that bring enough income to warrant the investments? In a way, most of us make a personal judgment concerning our own economic value when we determine how much life insurance we want to take out.

Inevitably the question arises whether one human life is worth more than another? Does our status in life or a specific skill we happen to possess sharply increase our economic value? Why does a soccer player merit millions of dollars? Should a top manager get millions in cash, shares, and share options when he leaves a business he has led for a few years, while someone else works faithfully for a company for 40 years and may get a thousand dollars extra when reaching retirement age? A few years ago a conference of development experts in Copenhagen discussed the economic value of human beings. A professor from Nottingham, England, suggested that the value of an American life could be put at approximately $6 million. People in the U.S. with risky jobs may demand an extra $60,000 for every percent their chances of having a fatal accident increase. So, Professor Appleton said, if 1 percent equals $60,000, 100 percent would amount to $6 million. On the other hand, the total life earnings of a worker in a developing country would average just over $22,000, and the economic value of such a person would therefore be limited to that amount!

Such reasoning may be flawed in several respects, but it illustrates the point. We place different values on human life, an impression confirmed in numerous ways. When we see the reports of war casualties in Iraq or Afghanistan, somehow we are much more concerned about a dozen dead soldiers of the Western coalition forces than 100 Iraqi or Afghan victims. And, of course, certain regimes seem to put an extremely low value on the life of some of their citizens and do not worry unduly if people suffer and die, as long as it does not put the interests of the rulers in danger.

Sometimes we measure the value of life in terms of its duration. Can a short life possibly have as much worth as a longer one? And are certain phases of life of more value than other periods? Society may regard young people as extra-valuable, because they still have a full life before them with a lot of potential still to be realized. Or is the mature person, with considerable experience, the most worthwhile? Some cultures tend to see seniors as of extra significance because of their wisdom, whereas in other societies we constantly hear about the great problems connected with the graying of the population and the added costs it brings in terms of health care, housing provisions, and ever higher benefit and pension payments.

A different perspective

Such questions will continue to surface, and each individual will answer differently. However, there is another perspective, and that is, thank God, the decisive one. It is quite simple: In the eyes of God every human being is a unique creature, but every human being has the same value. Many New Testament passages highlight this magnificent truth. One of the most entrancing illustrations is that of the good shepherd, who, while he carries a responsibility for the entire flock, will still do all he can to find and save the one sheep that has gone astray. Every individual can count on God's total interest in his or her situation. He does not go by numbers and averages or just by considering the bigger picture. God knows what happens to each one of us. Even the hairs on our head, a metaphor that is as touching as it is reassuring, tells us that they are numbered (Matt. 10:30). Our Creator does not measure the value of life in economic terms or in criteria of intellectual or artistic achievements. Disregarding the stage in the cycle of life that we are in, He has as much regard for children as for seniors, for women as for men. Nor does He measure worth by the length of a life. (Remember Christ

Himself lived only some 33 years, and His life was the "fullest" one ever lived!) Each individual human life is so precious in God's eyes that it is worth the ultimate sacrifice: the life of the Son of God.

Real life

Often we hear that if you have not seen this, been there, done that, etc., you have not really lived. What people mean to say is that real life is filled with excitement—that is, not dominated by dull routine and hedged in by a steady 9:00-to-5:00 pattern. Or they suggest that real life is lived outside of the protective circle of home and family. People must get a chance to experience the real world, with all its risks, its competitiveness and challenges. Only by exposure to the toughness of real life in the big, bad world does one become a real person, some will argue. But, defective though these viewpoints may be, they may be far less dangerous than the new trend that calls on people to escape from the any kind of real life into the virtual world of Second Life. Founded in 2003, this cyberworld has grown explosively and now has millions of "inhabitants" from many different countries. Those who log in on their computer and enter it can become avatars and lead a virtual life in which they can buy and sell with Linden dollars. They can meet people, enjoy all kinds of entertainments, find information, travel, buy and furnish a home, and even go to church. Yes, it is "only" a game. But it is an enslaving way to withdraw from the realities of real life, and it poses the very real threat that many will find it increasingly difficult to separate fact from fiction.

Returning to the question as to what "real life" is, the Christian answer is the most satisfying. The definition can be quite short. *Real life is life in Christ.* This real life starts after one has been reborn. It differs radically from the life that is naturally ours. "Humans can reproduce only human life, but the Holy Spirit gives new life from heaven" (John 3:6). The apostle Paul had experienced this dramatic change and could testify: "I myself no longer live, but Christ lives in me. So I live my life in this earthly body by trusting in the Son of God" (Gal. 2:20). He encourages all who will listen to him to follow his example. "Clothe yourselves with the armor of right living, as those who live in the light," he says (Rom. 13:12). In other words: "Let the Lord Jesus take control of you" (verse 14).

The new life is, in essence, eternal. It may have a temporary interruption when we die, but this kind of death is not the end. We belong to Christ and have the certainty of eternity. "If we have hope in Christ only for this life," we have not understood what the gospel means, and "we are the most miserable people in the world" (1 Cor. 15:19). "The free gift of God" is not just a satisfying life in the present (even though it is this as well), but it "is eternal life through Christ Jesus our Lord" (Rom. 6:23). It is a reality because Christ is a reality. And it is available to all who choose to accept it. "This is the way to have eternal life—to know you, the only true God, and Jesus Christ, the one you sent to earth" (John 17:3).

The Christian life is not always an easy one. We can describe Christian living as a process of "fighting the good fight," which requires us "to hold tightly to the eternal life" (1 Tim. 6:12). It is a disciplined life,[4] a truly purpose-driven life,[5] and, most definitely, an enjoyable life as well. The wise man advises us: "Eat your food and drink your wine with a happy heart, for God approves of this! Wear fine clothes, with a dash of cologne!" (Eccl. 9:7). "Enjoy your work and accept your lot in life—that is indeed a gift from God" (Eccl. 5:19). "I recommend having fun," he adds in Ecclesiastes 8:15. How much clearer can he be? Yet the same wise man also urges balance and stresses that there is a time for everything (see Eccl. 3:1).

The art of Christian living is truly a balancing act. It requires spiritual insight and growth.[6] How can you learn to be assertive without being aggressive? How can you overcome fear without being foolhardy? How do you master the art of showing mercy without condoning wrong and of giving freely without giving yourself away? How do you become strong without being rigid or optimistic without being unrealistic?

Real life has a dual dimension. First, it is focused on this world, on the joys of this earth, on the relationships that one can develop and the services that one can render. It is far from escapist or otherworldly. Yet at the same time it is also fully centered on the life to come and on preparing for eternity. For many it is hard to understand how to integrate both orientations into one purpose-driven life successfully. The only way in which this is possible, is if the two perspectives have one single focal point: Jesus Christ—the source of life. But let's not be too surprised if many people around us fail to fathom what this means. After all, it is a spiritual matter, and, unfortunately, "people who aren't Christians can't understand these truths from God's Spirit. It all sounds foolish to them because only those who have the Spirit can understand what the Spirit means" (1 Cor. 2:14)!

---

[1] *Origins—A Skeptic's Guide to the Creation of Life on Earth* (1986), p. 128. See www.allaboutthejourney.org/miracle-of-life.htm.

[2] See www.allaboutthejourney.org/miracle-of-life.htm.

[3] Ellen G. White, *The Desire of Ages*, p. 530.

[4] Richard J. Foster's *The Challenge of the Disciplined Life: Christian Reflections on Money, Sex and Power* (San Francisco: Harper and Row, 1985) remains an excellent book about this aspect of the life of a Christian.

[5] Whether or not one agrees with all of the content of Rick Warren's bestseller, the title *The Purpose Driven Life* certainly encapsulates what a Christian life should be.

[6] This paragraph is a very brief summary of a very useful book by Ray S. Anderson, *Living the Spiritually Balanced Life* (Grand Rapids: Baker Books, 1998).

REVELATION 5

"Revelation is . . . a manifestation of God's grace. It involves an enormous condescension on God's part to stoop to the level where finite, rebellious human beings can hear his message. We might say that God lisps when He talks to us, just as an affectionate parent uses baby talk to communicate with a very young child."

—RICHARD RICE, *Reign of God,* p. 25

Entering the forecourt of the ancient temple of Apollo, the Greek god of the sun, in Delphi, the ancient worshipper would read the famous words "Know Thyself." These words, attributed to at least five different Greek sages, have inspired people throughout the centuries to engage in serious introspection. Christians will fully agree that knowing ourselves—our own motives, possibilities, and limitations—is an important aspect of being a responsible human being. Yet, for Christians, that is not where it starts or ends. Beyond just knowing ourselves, and as a precondition to real self-knowledge, they will seek to know God, the one in whom, they believe, we "live and move and exist" (Acts 17:28). And this—knowing God— becomes the believer's first and most fundamental concern.

This immediately raises all kinds of questions. Is it, in fact, possible to know God? Even if we are convinced that He exists, do we have ways of getting close enough to Him that we may proceed beyond mere speculation to a true knowledge of who and what He is? If so, how much can we know? For surely, if we are dealing with a God who is infinite, our finite mind must of necessity soon confront barriers beyond which it cannot penetrate. And if we can indeed know something of and about God, what kind of knowledge might it be? Are we talking about the kind of rational knowledge that expresses itself in theological and philosophical formulas, or rather about a mystical and intuitive awareness that finds its primary expression in feelings and emotions?

From above or from below?

A few years ago a Dutch theologian wrote a book with a rather surprising title: *God Is So Great That He Does Not Need to Exist*. The author, Professor Gerrit Manenschijn, claims what many other theologians have also concluded: When we speak of God, we express our own thoughts. It is human thinking—and no more, deep and innovative and insightful as it may be. Everything we say about heavenly things actually comes from below. All God talk is human speech. And that will have to do. In fact, this should make us more than happy, for it provides us with enough spiritual guidance for our life in this world. It is all that we need and may hope for. Everything beyond our present world and our human existence is unknowable. Any theology (knowledge of God) that is useful to us and moves beyond mere speculation is, in actual fact, a form of anthropology (knowledge of humanity). And thus, these theologians have led us back to the pagan temple of Delphi, where knowledge of ourselves is the highest spiritual and academic ambition that we may cherish.

Of course, what many contemporary theologians, who deny the reality of divine revelation (for that is what their reasoning, however learned and cleverly packaged, amounts to) argue echoes the theories of Sigmund Freud, the founder of the school of psychoanalysis, and of the (in)famous Friedrich Nietzsche—two of the key figures at the basis of the mode of thinking usually referred to as postmodernism. Freud claimed that all talk about God as our heavenly Father is, in actual fact, no more than a reaction to our mostly subconscious sentiments with regard to our human father! Our convictions about God therefore simply are creations of our own minds.

Postmodern philosophers are obsessed with language and its role in our lives. Many of them argue that our words can indeed be useful symbols for communication. Each community assigns a particular meaning to its jargon, and so members of a given community may understand each other. But that does not mean that these words do actually refer to something that has a real existence apart from the words themselves. To say it in the technical terms they mostly use: words do not necessarily have a referent—that is something real, something objective and independent to which they refer. Each community has its own "language game" and invents its own words. Theological language, they propose, is one such language game. It is useful for people who belong to a particular religious community. When they talk about God, there is a shared use of language. But minds that function in a certain way, within a certain context, have invented the words. This does not, however, of itself point to any reality beyond these words.

Communication from "above" to "below"

To accept the concept of divine revelation is therefore more and more a matter of going against the tide. Believing in revelation in the true—biblical—sense is the opposite of maintaining that everything that speaks of "things above" comes from "below." The concept of revelation implies that there is "Someone" who makes it possible for those "below" to have a real (if limited) understanding of "things above." It also implies that it is not a luxury that we could do just as well without. We do not really discover *who* we are unless we first find out *whose* we are and what we can become.

In affirming the possibility of revelation we should be careful, however, not to obliterate the infinite difference between the Creator and the creature. When medieval mystics sought to take their mystical devotion, often combined with physical deprivation, to absurd extremes in their belief that they could eventually achieve a form of oneness with the divine, they suffered from a serious misapprehension. The gap between God and humanity is and remains infinite. Any revelation will therefore always be partial and limited. The full light of God's presence would not be helpful —it would actually be lethal. No story in the Bible is as clear on this point as is the account of Moses' desire to see the infinite God. Moses was eager to receive a full and final assurance that God would be with him as the leader of His people. His pleadings with

God to give him the absolute certainty that he was craving for, culminated in his ultimate plea: "Please let me see your glorious presence" (Ex. 33:18). God wanted his servant to have the assurance he wanted, but could oblige only to a very limited extent. "You may not look directly at my face," the Lord said, "for no one may see me and live" (verse 20). Then follows a passage that may at first sound a little strange, but the basic message is clear: "The Lord continued, 'Stand here on this rock beside me. As my glorious presence passes by, I will put you in the cleft of the rock and cover you with my hand until I have passed. Then I will remove my hand, and you will see me from behind. But my face will not be seen'" (verses 21-23). This magnificent if somewhat mystifying story contains a vital truth about the ways in which God reveals Himself. Revelation is, one might say, an unveiling, but not in any total or absolute sense. "The revealed things belong to us and our descendants forever," but "there are secret things that belong to the Lord our God" (Deut. 29:29).

In various ways

The author of the Epistle to the Hebrews begins his letter (maybe "sermon" is a better word) with the matter-of-fact statement that "long ago God spoke many times and in many ways to our ancestors." At first, He spoke through the prophets, but later ("in these final days") He "has spoken to us through his Son" (Heb. 1:1). The apostle Paul adds a particular dimension of God's method of revelation. Nature around us, he says, is not just for our use or enjoyment. For, looking with the right kind of eyes, we "can clearly see" God's "invisible qualities—his eternal power and divine nature" (Rom. 1:20).

To many who already have come to believe in God, "the book of nature" is indeed a fabulously illustrated commentary on God's creative power. When they look at a starry sky, see a mighty river, marvel at the glittering snow on the top of a majestic mountain, wonder at the countless colors of a Pacific coral reef, or peer through a microscope at marvels that remain hidden to the naked eye; when they hear the rolling thunder, experience the vast emptiness of the desert or listen to the symphony of the birds that untiringly sing their songs, they are convinced that they see irrefutable evidence of the omnipotence of the Creator. It has also happened that men and women, who did not previously have a real faith in God, experienced a sudden flash of insight when confronted with an uncommon natural phenomenon or had a sudden realization of the majesty of nature around them. Christians tend to agree with the apostle Paul that an honest, unbiased inspection of nature should set people thinking. Can anyone really attribute everything around us to the aftermath of a "big bang"? Is this really the most convincing suggestion or theory? (For that is what it is: a hypothesis that rests on unproven presuppositions.) Or does nature rather point us toward some form of intelligent design? Is a theistic approach (one that involves a powerful God) at least as probable as one that refuses to allow for such a possibility?

When all this is said and done, it is, however, clear that nature can at the most only provide a very partial answer to all the questions we have about God. The book of nature also contains many pages of terrible cruelty. Who has not at some time watched with dismay, or even with disgust, a television documentary that showed in gory detail how animals kill without mercy? How can we reconcile the horrendous cruelty in nature with the idea of a loving Creator? Through the ages the beauty of the human body has inspired countless works of great art. After all, God made humanity but "a little lower than the angels" (Ps. 8:5). Yet little of that beauty remains when disease robs the body not only of its strength but all too often also of its dignity.

And what about the death and destruction caused, in ever-increasing frequency and scope, it seems, by tsunamis, floods, forest fires, earthquakes, and other natural phenomena? Would we not expect an omnipotent God to be in better control of nature? How do we reconcile the reality of the deadly forces of nature that ruin the lives of millions of men, women, children, and livestock with faith in a God of love and mercy? Such questions would remain insolvable if we had no additional source or Source of revelation.

The Written Word

That source of additional information about God is Scripture. Anyone who knows anything about the Bible realizes that it is a unique book. Almost 40 different authors produced it during a period of more than 1,500 years. Its writers, with all their diversity in educational, cultural, and occupational background, employed a wide scope of literary styles. The book has provided great comfort and immense spiritual support to the uneducated, but has at the same time been the subject of continuing academic research. Naturally it stands to reason that it would be a unique book, if it is what it claims: Gods Word in human languages. Two basic elements must be kept in balance, but should each get their full weight. 1. The Bible is the vehicle through which *God speaks* to us. It is not humans addressing fellow humans. 2. It is *God speaking through fellow humans* to us. God, in His grace, stoops to our level. He cannot communicate to us in the same way He does with heavenly beings. Rather, He gracefully accepts the limitations of human words, of human reasoning and human stories. God chose to reveal what He wanted us to know and understand employing ancient Hebrew and a particular kind of Greek, with a smattering of Aramaic. The Bible is therefore simultaneously divine and human. That is its true uniqueness.

God has left it to us to translate, as best as we can, this unique collection of 66 "books" into English and French and Chinese and whatever other languages we can read and understand. The task of retelling the Word in the kind of language that people of different cultures and with varying educational levels and ages may understand remains an ongoing challenge. We must always remember that the Bible does not really become the Word of God for us until we can hear it in a language that we can understand.

Its readers and listeners must focus on the real intention of God's communication to us. Although we find a lot of trustworthy historical information in the Bible, it is not primarily a history textbook. And even though the Bible is the foundational text for all theological endeavors, it is not designed as a one-volume systematic theology. The Bible's primary purpose is to help us—

human beings—to establish and strengthen our relationship with God, and thus to find meaning, structure, and direction for our lives.

The Spirit of God inspired the biblical authors (2 Tim. 3:16). The Holy Spirit "moved the prophets to speak from God" (2 Peter 1:21). They did thereby not become a mechanical pen, moved by a mysterious unseen power, recording words produced without the involvement of their own minds and without any impact from the world in which they lived. It would be more correct to say that the "thoughts" of the Bible are inspired rather than the individual words. Strangely enough, the theory of verbal inspiration (that God personally selected every word in the original text of the Bible) has always had its supporters, also among Seventh-day Adventists, in spite of the clear evidence to the contrary. Ellen White was quite clear about what she believed. In 1886, while visiting Europe, she wrote: "The Bible is written by inspired men, but it is not God's mode of thought and expression. It is that of humanity. God, as a writer, is not represented. . . . God has not put Himself in words, in logic, in rhetoric, on trial in the Bible. The writers of the Bible were God's penmen, not His pen. Look at the different writers. It is not the words of the Bible that are inspired, but the men that were inspired. Inspiration acts not on the man's words or his expressions but on the man himself, who, under the influence of the Holy Ghost, is imbued with thoughts. But the words receive the impress of the individual mind. The divine mind is diffused. The divine mind and will is combined with the human mind and will; thus the utterances of the man are the word* of God."*

In their search for words to express as clearly as possible the message the Spirit wanted them to convey, the authors of the Bible often used analogies and metaphors. By focusing on certain aspects of persons, objects, or phenomena and applying them to their subject, they hoped to create fresh insights for the reader or listener. For instance, by comparing God to a shepherd, who cares for his sheep with total commitment, David has helped millions of readers of the twenty-third Psalm to catch a glimpse of God's care for His human creatures. Of course we understand that, while God is *like* the shepherd in certain respects, He is totally *unlike* the shepherd in many other aspects! Nonetheless, truth is conveyed very effectively. Christ was the absolute master in using metaphors to explain to His disciples what He wanted them to know. Time and again, He would start out with "The kingdom of heaven is like . . ." and then zoom in on something that would illustrate a particular aspect of the coming kingdom in a much more effective way than a barrage of abstract language would have done.

The Bible authors used poetry and apocalyptic imagery and several other stylistic forms, but for most readers, past and present, the *story* may well be the most appealing format. The Bible stories are true stories, but they do far more than just provide information—historical, biographical, or otherwise. They do that as well, but always from a certain perspective. Look at the stories of Israel's kings. Although they are historically trustworthy, they are also incomplete and subjective. They relate only certain things, and those kings who "did what was good in the eyes of the Lord" tend to get more extensive coverage than those who did evil, even if such rulers sometimes were of greater political importance. Their story is part of salvation history. That is the perspective that counts. The creation story is a true account of the origin of our planet and life on it. It is, however, far from complete and leaves many loose ends, leaving us wondering exactly how some things fit together. While we concentrate in our search for *what* the story tells us, we must, however, not overlook *why* the story is told in the way it is and must look for the *spiritual message* behind the facts. What does it mean that God is our Creator and what does it imply that He created you and me in His image? Take another example: Why does the apostle John tell us about only seven miracles, although Christ performed many, many more? And why did he choose the particular ones he included? What John tells us has actually happened. But surely it was not all that happened. Why did he make this particular selection? We must largely guess why the Spirit led him to make his particular choice, but the careful student may discern an interesting theological pattern. And we could add hundreds of examples in which we see humanity's creative involvement in the choice of the stories and the words that channel the divine Word.

We will never be able to explain fully how inspiration works. The miraculous blending of the perfect activity of the divine Spirit with that of the creative, but limited and imperfect, involvement of the human spirit is beyond our understanding. Theories of inspiration cannot do justice to such a miracle and tend to be out of balance. They either emphasize the divine or the human element too much—or too little. An overemphasis on the divine leaves us with an unbiblical theory, while an overemphasis on the human element robs the Holy Scriptures of their divine authority. Also, let us not forget that the role of the Holy Spirit is not limited to the *production* of the Bible. If we are to profit from its *reading*, the Spirit must likewise be constantly involved. Unless the Spirit aids our understanding, the words remain empty—in fact, they remain only human—and fail to become a revelation, and as such "a lamp to [our] feet and a light for [our] path" (Ps. 119:105, NIV).

Seeing God

The Bible reveals aspects of God and of His plan of salvation that nature cannot disclose, but even the Written Word was not adequate. In "the final days" God, therefore, took a giant leap forward in His dealings with humanity. Not only did He give the Word to us in human language, but He also provided humanity with a picture of flesh and blood. God's "unfailing love and faithfulness" became visible in his Son, who "became human and lived here on earth among us" (John 1:14). By looking at Him we see what God is like. He said: "Anyone who has seen me has seen the Father" (John 14:9).

God becoming human ("becoming flesh," as some translations put it)—this is the limit to which God can go. Further revelations will have to wait, until He lifts us above our present limitations. "Now we see things imperfectly as in a poor mirror, but then we will see everything with perfect clarity " (1 Cor. 13:12).

Aspects of revelation

This short chapter can touch on only a few aspects of this fabulous theme of revelation. But let me make some important points for your further consideration:

1. Allow me to repeat what I stated earlier: What God reveals tells us something real about Him, even though many things will still remain hidden. Revelation truly comes from above and not from below! Scholars who believe this use a technical term to underline this. They deny that speaking about God is no more than a language game, but are adamant that God talk has a *referent*, that is, that it refers to a reality that exists independently of what we say about it. Yet human words can never fully define heavenly realities.

2. To use another technical term: revelation is *accommodational*. God employs *human* words—the kind of words and images people used at a particular time, within a specific context. Recognizing this is essential if we, who live at a later time and within a different cultural context, want to understand the meaning of what God intends to tell us. At the same time, however, we must beware that we do not fall into the trap of reducing everything to a mere reflection of culture and historical context. A timeless message always awaits us beneath the cultural wrappings of the time in which the biblical authors wrote.

3. Divine revelation took place within a particular *community*. In most cases, the attempts at understanding what God disclosed also happen within a community context. The community has its own history, its own traditions, and its own jargon. It would be naive to suggest that the community of which we are part does not affect the way that we read the Word of God and explain its meaning for us today. Adventists do not come to the Bible with their mind as a tabula rasa. They cannot avoid reading their Bible with certain Adventist presuppositions in line with the tradition to which they belong. The challenge every community—including the Adventist community—has to face constantly is whether it can remain objective enough toward its own traditions and stay willing to move beyond them in the pursuit of "more light."

4. Receiving God's revelation requires *theological reflection*. In

order to get a better grip on what He seeks to tell us, we may need words and symbols that are not part of the biblical vocabulary. The Bible does not employ such words and expressions as Trinity, persons of the Godhead, natures of Christ. Nor does it refer to divine attributes, such as omnipotence, omniscience, etc. Most Christians have agreed that such words are useful in systematizing our limited understanding of what God has revealed about Himself. But let us not forget: these (and many other) terms are human words that can at best point only to aspects of the truth, without ever providing a full description of it. And many of these words carry their own baggage. For instance, the word "person," when first introduced into the Christian theological vocabulary, meant something quite different from what many consider it to signify today.

5. An unbiased approach to the Scriptures will lead us to the conclusion that God's method of using human "penmen" has resulted in a *trustworthy, but not totally error-free,* text. One interesting example of this appears in 2 Samuel 24 and in 1 Chronicles 23. Both passages relate the story of David's census of the people. It is clearly the same story in outline, but not in every detail. Even the result of the head count is not quite the same in the two renderings. We are, however, not to worry about such things. Inspiration apparently works in such a way that it does not eliminate or avoid minor discrepancies, such as we find in this example. But we do not need to have any doubt about what the message is.

6. Finally, revelation is *progressive.* The prophets built on the books of Moses. The New Testament builds on the Old. The revelation through Christ surpasses everything else that went before. But although we have a clear progression, it never means that what God has revealed previously is now obsolete or inconclusive. The Lord will disclose even more to us in the world to come. The fact that what has already been revealed to us may be limited does not, however, indicate that it remains inconclusive and insufficient for our spiritual journey. But given our humanness, with all its limitations, it does mean that there will always exist the challenge of probing deeper into what God has revealed—individually and as a

community. Our understanding of what God has opened to us is also progressive. We will always have more to see and understand. There is always room for further growth "in the knowledge of our Lord and Saviour Jesus Christ" (2 Peter 3:18). And when we speak of this kind of knowledge, we must remember what true "knowledge" is in the biblical sense: not primarily propositional data deposited in formulas, proofs, and arguments, but relational knowledge. For in the end, that is what God's revelation is all about: a guide to a personal relationship with God.

---

* Ellen G. White, *Selected Messages,* book 1, p. 21. For another classic statement about Ellen White's view on inspiration, see the introduction of *The Great Controversy.*

SIN 6

"There are sins of omission, as well as sins of commission, and all of us are influencing the course of others. A neglect when the work is laid before you is as wrong as to perform some sinful action, for in neglecting your duty you fail to supply your link in the chain of God's great work."

—ELLEN G. WHITE, *Manuscript Releases*, vol. 11, p. 297

"And it isn't the thing you do, dear,
It's the thing you leave undone
Which gives you heartache
At the setting of the sun."

—MARGARET E. SANGSTER

Sin" is one of those common words that have suffered from constant devaluation. People use it in all kinds of settings and at times even attach a positive connotation of adventure and fun to it. Often they especially link it to exciting sexual behavior, or to various forms of overindulgence, which may be unwise but are nonetheless painted as understandable or even enjoyable. In this chapter we will look at the true meaning of the term and see how the Bible defines it, and what "sin" means to the Christian who seeks to emulate the Sinless One.

Questions

The Bible defines sin as opposition to the law of God (1 John 3:4). At first sight this appears to be rather simple. You consult the law, and whatever is not in agreement with it is sin. But what law is John referring to? The ten-commandment law? Or is there a broader application to other laws and injunctions? And even if we focus on the Ten Commandments, what are the implications of Jesus' teachings? Did He not tell His disciples that the impact of this divine law extends far beyond the immediate literal application, but includes inner motives as well (see Matt. 5:27)?

Other issues may be even more difficult to handle. We realize that theft is wrong, or "sinful," as a Christian would say. If I steal a BMW because I am not content with the car I have, I commit a sin. Or if I steal $100,000 by defrauding the company for which I work, I am a thief. But what if I have absolutely no money (through no fault of my own) and take a loaf of bread, simply to stay alive? Does that also fall into the same category of sin? And what if I am a kleptomaniac, someone utterly unable to resist the impulse of stealing? I am not stealing because I want to have all kinds of luxury items. Instead, I take small things of little value, forced by some strange, inner compulsion beyond my control. Does this make me a thief—or a patient in need of therapy?

People usually consider murder the worst possible type of sin. In our scale of values a wide chasm looms between telling a white lie and willfully stabbing our neighbor to death after a confrontation about the amount of decibels coming from his or her house. But is physical violence in principle more objectionable than verbal abuse? And is murdering two people intrinsically more evil than killing just one person? Is a serial killer more evil than someone who kills just once or twice? Or may mass murderers be actually less culpable, if we discover that they suffer from some inner compulsion that has starkly reduced their personal responsibility?

Other questions arise, as soon as we begin to think about sin. Is there something called "original" sin, or "hereditary" or "ancestral" sin? A concept that has found its way into Christian theology, it refers to the general condition of sinfulness into which all human beings are born, rather than to actual acts of sin. One might compare it to a virus that has stealthily infected the world after the first human couple "fell" into sin. Church Father Augustine, and others after him, suggested that infant baptism is required to deal with the lethal result of original sin. If an unbaptized child dies, its sinful condition destines it for hell. Apart from the fact that this view of hell sadly lacks biblical substance, the concept of original sin also has other indefensible elements. Nevertheless, the question remains: Why do we start out in life with such a serious disadvantage because of the mistake of our first parents? What justice is there in the fact that "Adam's sin brought death" and that, as a result, "death spread to everyone" and that "Adam's one sin brought condemnation upon everyone" (Rom. 5:12, 18)?

What is sin?

We could add additional questions to those posed in the previous paragraph. The text just quoted from Romans 5 suggests a principle of causality. One thing is caused by the other, thus setting a chain of events in motion. One sin tragically led to universal sin, and universal sin resulted in universal death. There is truth in that. Yet we must be careful not to talk only in terms of causality, as if every specific problem, and every specific case of human suffering, is the product of an identifiable sin on the part of a specific individual. Remember the biblical story of the man born blind? Jesus' disciples, who were used to such thinking in terms of cause and effect, asked, "Teacher, why was this man born blind? Was it a result of his own sins or of those of his parents?" (see John 9:2). Jesus told them not to make such rash connections. "It was not because of his sins or of his parents' sins. He was born blind so the power of God could be seen in him" (see verse 3). Jesus also underlined this truth when He referred to an incident that had caused the death of 18 men. The Tower of Siloam had collapsed and buried 18 victims under its debris. "Were they the worst sinners in Jerusalem?" Jesus asked (Luke 13:4). Clearly He did not want people to draw that conclusion and link their accidental death with any specific sinful behavior. Things are more complex than that. Bad things happen to bad people, but they happen to good people as well.

While there is *personal* sin, there is also *corporate* sin. Sin has infected the world, and as a result, the world finds itself subject to death and decay. Humanity has become enslaved to sin (see Rom. 6). We saw in the chapter on "revelation" that God's creation suffers under the effects of sin. "We know," the apostle Paul affirms, "that all creation has been groaning as in the pains of childbirth right up to the present time" (Rom. 8:22).

Individual responsibility and corporate responsibility are connected. Because many of us make wrong choices, events in the world take a certain turn and a kind of society develops in which humanity, rather than God, is the measure of all things. Because lots of individual people do not control their greediness and egotism, the world gets characterized by materialism and self-centeredness. At the same time, the kind of selfish and violent world humanity has "created" will influence all who now are born into it. And this cancer of sins keeps on metastasizing with unstoppable results. However, we cannot just blame our upbringing, the environment, our genes, or whatever else. In the Bible sin is more than an infection that has spread and now holds all of us captive. The primary biblical definition of sin refers to conscious sinful behavior. "All wrongdoing is sin," we read in 1 John 5:17 (NIV). Most Bible translations speak of "unrighteousness" as the main element of sin. When we sin, we oppose the law of God (see 1 John 3:4). Sin is not going against some vague ideal or general principle, but is nothing less than outright rebellion against God. David recognized this when he meditated upon his adulterous past: "Against you, and you alone, have I sinned" (Ps. 51:4). Note that sin has to do with an act of will. It is going against a norm, the absolute law of God. This differs radically from what most postmodern people believe. For them no absolute rules exist. We are, they maintain, only dealing with individual preferences and a consensus that has developed in society. While we may not like certain things, that does not make them inherently evil. Even though we may feel the need for personal growth and may regard some things in our own conduct as weaknesses that we would like to outgrow, all this falls far short of the biblical view of sin as willful, active rebellion against an absolute law given by a divine lawgiver. "Sin is the transgression of the law." Once again I quote 1 John 3:4, but this time in the old King James Version. This translation even more poignantly underlines how God defines a boundary for humanity. God says that sin is transgressing His holy, spiritual law (Rom. 7:12-14). Breaking that law—crossing that divine boundary, the limit God set for us—is sin.

The medieval Christian regarded seven sins as being in a category of their own. The "deadly" sins (also known as the "cardinal" sins) required special sacramental action if forgiveness and absolution was to be obtained. We meet them for the first time in a sixth-century list, that originated with Pope Gregory the Great (c. 540-604): lust, gluttony, greed, sloth, anger, envy, and pride. Each sin corresponds with a particular virtue: chastity, abstinence, liberality, diligence, patience, kindness, and humility. We find no biblical foundation for a distinction between "cardinal" and lesser, "venial" sins. And this medieval list, and any other lists that we might compile, of sins that supposedly are more serious than other wrongdoings, may mislead us more than they help, because they may suggest that some sins are actually less serious than others! However, the traditional list of deadly sins does suggest that attitude and motive play an important role. It is a clear biblical principle that Christ Himself strongly emphasized. Lusting after someone's wife or indulging in sexual fantasies is just as sinful as a full-blown adulterous relationship, and being obsessed by hateful feelings is not intrinsically different from the actual pulling of the trigger (Matt. 5:21-28).

But we do not exhaust the phenomenon of sin by stating that sin is an act of willful transgression of a holy law that has been revealed to us for our guidance through life, or the nurturing of a desire to commit such a transgression, if only one had the guts to do so. James 4:17 adds a significant aspect: "Remember, it is sin to know what you ought to do and then not do it." So in addition to the sins of *commission*, there also exist sins of *omission*. Jesus' parable of Lazarus and the rich man (Luke 16:19-31) provides a prime example of this type of sin. The story tells us that the rich man bitterly complained about his fate in the hereafter to "father" Abraham, comparing his own misery to the bliss the poor beggar was experiencing. God explains through Abraham that the rich man could have done things in his earthly life, that he failed to do. Those omissions now come to haunt him. The passage of Matthew 25:31-46 contains the same moral. When Jesus returns "with his reward," things that we have failed to do may be the reason we lose eternal life.

It takes but little thought to realize that all kinds of things happen because people failed to act. Edmund Burke (Irish statesman and philosopher, 1729-1797) has been credited with observing that "all that is needed for evil to triumph is for good people to do nothing."

Yet "sin" stretches even further. Its meaning also covers the idea of "missing the mark." This is the root meaning of one of the most frequently used Greek words (*hamartia*) and its Hebrew equivalents that translators render as "sin." "You are to be perfect as your Father in heaven is perfect" (Matt. 5:48). If the goal is to reach perfection, it will always be beyond our reach. "All have sinned; all fall short of God's glorious standard" (Rom. 3:23). Of course, such "missing the mark" is a reality that we constantly meet in our daily lives. In so many ways we fall short of the ideals we profess to uphold; so many ways in which we disappoint others and ourselves as we fail to meet promises that we should have kept and goals that we should have reached but didn't.

The reality of sin

Without doubt sin is a crucial theme in the Christian vocabulary. We must approach it with utter seriousness, never pushing its stark reality aside or toning it down. Naturally, we wonder about the origin of sin. The Genesis story of the Fall tells us about the first human act of rebellion. It seemed like a minor thing: picking a fruit that looked appealing and appetizing. But it was nothing less than the first demonstration of human hubris, exchanging God's standards for own own.

How could it happen? Because God had created humanity with the freedom of choice. Human beings could remain obedient or could, on the other hand, choose to follow their own way. They could listen to the voice of their Creator or to the deceptive suggestions of the evil one. Prior to the Fall in Paradise a heavenly confrontation between good and evil had already taken place. A heavenly being had exercised his power of choice and had chosen to rebel, and had found a following among the angelic beings. A number of biblical passages provide us with a glimpse of what happened (see Rev. 12:7-13; Eze. 28:12-19; Isa. 14:12-14).

As soon as God created humanity, Satan, the captain of the evil angels, did what he could to infect the newly created earth with the germ of sin. And with success. We cannot fully understand the what and why of this "fall" into sin? It remains, in a very real sense, a mystery. The term used in 2 Thessalonians 2:7 is very apt: the "mystery of iniquity" (KJV).

For many reasons the theory of evolution is inadequate as an explanation of origins. One key problem that the evolutionary hypothesis cannot solve is that of the origin of moral judgment, of distinguishing between good and evil. Evolutionary thinking has no place for sin as a moral transgression of a divine law, and of any moral shortcomings of omission—of "missing" some moral mark. The evolutionist reduces sin to a stage of development, a skill that must yet be mastered or an insight yet to be gained as everything develops through long periods of time. There is no moral injunction to protect the weak. In fact, the weak must of necessity lose out, so that "the fittest" may survive. Many often argue that the Christian faith has nothing to fear from the theory of evolution. Yes, it is maintained, we must abandon a literal reading of the Bible as outdated and prescientific, but the deeper truth of the Christian religion is not in any real danger. Nothing could, however, be further from the truth. Evolution is irreconcilable with the reality of sin. Evolutionists don't need a Savior—they just require more time to develop further. Thus those who want to integrate the biblical message with evolutionary thought must excise the biblical Christ from Christianity.

But sin is a reality that demands a lifelong battle. It is a conflict with superhuman dimensions. "We are not fighting against people of flesh and blood, but against the evil rulers and authorities of the unseen world" (Eph. 6:12). In this struggle we need all the protection and weapons that we can possibly line up. Scripture admonishes us to be "strong with the Lord's mighty power" (verse 10). The advice is straightforward: "Put on all of God's armor so that you will be able to stand firm against all strategies and tricks of the Devil" (verse 11). Our fight is, first of all, against our personal sin. We may be struggling against our tendency to be rather economical with the truth. Some of us easily erupt in anger. Many sense the temptation of pride and prejudice. Others of us may suffer from an addiction that, again and again, proves too strong for us to master. Sin takes a multitude of forms. Once we truly realize this, we will cease to be judgmental about others who may be battling against sins that we do not personally wrestle with. Every one of us has a personal struggle. It has always been a mystery to me how some Christians have dared to conclude that they have fully mastered sin. First John 1:10 leaves no room for that assessment: "If we claim we have not sinned, we are calling God a liar and showing that his word has no place in our hearts." Christ spoke to us as much as as He did to the Jewish leaders who eagerly condemned the behavior of the woman who was "caught in the act," when He said: "Let those who have never sinned throw the first stones" (John 8:7). (Adventist teachings about the time of the end include the expectation that as part of the final events Christ's mediation shall cease and the remnant believers will have to survive without their Mediator. In our present situation we do not know how this will be possible. Let us, in any case—taking into consideration the full biblical definition of sin—not conclude from this that in our present condition any of us can reach a state of sinlessness. "If we say we have no sin, we are only fooling ourselves" [1 John 1:8].)

Our warfare against sin definitely includes corporate sin. Neither as individuals, nor as a church community, can we passively accept that our world is evil. Whatever influence we may have we must use to reduce the violence in this world and the materialistic culture of waste and exploitation. Christians cannot simply accept as a deplorable but unalterable fact that 12-year-old children are enlisted as soldiers, that women are beaten and abused, and that HIV-sufferers do not get the medicines that science has made available. The conviction of Christ's soon return, when He will finally eradicate all evil, cannot lead to a complacent laissez-faire and a refusal to help the needy and the hungry as much as we can. As long as we live in this world we continue to be the light of the world and the salt of the earth (Matt. 5:13-16).

How successful can we hope to be?

The fight against sin is never fully over as long is we are citizens of the present world. The fact that we will remain sinners as long as we live, does, however, not mean that we cannot gain any victories. Christians know from experience that "there is power, power, wonder-working power, in the precious blood of the Lamb."*

Overcoming sin is always a matter of grace—a gift from God. We will take a closer look at this in the next chapter. But God does expect things of us if we want grace to have its influence on us. For a start, we can determine to avoid compromising situations, to stay away from places or events that may tempt us to do something that we know we should not do. If alcohol is a problem, we had better not frequent places in which it is in ample supply. Should we struggle with the problem of Internet pornography, putting the PC in a place that all can see what is on the screen in front of us may be a useful preventive measure. Or if our fight is against laziness, we would do well to commit ourselves to some structured activity and ask someone to monitor us. We must try to replace activities that affect us in a negative way with others that strengthen positive attitudes and awaken positive desires. "Don't let evil get the best of you, but conquer evil by doing good" (Rom. 12:21).

Sometimes we need outside help. Overcoming certain addictions may well require specialized treatment. In addition to any willpower we might be able to muster, we often require treatment and assistance that will give a new direction to our lives. In general, encouragement from others will help to deal with our weaknesses. There are friends who can take us down the path of destruction, but some friends can be more valuable than blood brothers (see Prov. 18:24).

And then there is prayer. And more prayer. Prayer for God to help us to resist temptation (Matt. 6:13). Prayer to help us be strong when pressure to sin comes our way unexpectedly. Prayer for deliverance when the devil seeks to "devour" us (1 Peter 5:8). Prayer to persevere. And, of course, prayer for forgiveness. And then for even more forgiveness.

Guilt

As we close this chapter we need to highlight one particular aspect: We cannot get rid of all our sin and sinfulness. Sin will keep raising its ugly head. But we do not need to continue to suffer from guilt. Our guilt can be taken away from us—totally. That is what atonement is all about—what it means when we say that we are "saved." The glorious truth is that there exists a satisfying answer to the question once asked by the apostle Paul and ever since repeated from the lips of millions of Christians: "Oh, what a miserable person I am! Who will free me from this life that is dominated by sin?" What better assurance can there be than Paul's conclusion: "Thank God! The answer is in Jesus Christ our Lord" (Rom. 7:24, 25). Human effort will never solve the dilemma of sin. But there is a solution. We have a Savior.

---

* Music and words of this song ("Power in the Blood") by Lewis E. Jones (1899).

"A grace-full Christian is one who looks at the world through 'grace-tinted lenses.'"

—PHILIP YANCEY, *What's So Amazing About Grace?* p. 272

When Paul came to the Greek city of Corinth, he wondered what approach he should use to reach his audience. Finally he decided to put all his eggs in one basket. He did not go for the "lofty words and brilliant ideas" his creative mind might be able to produce, but instead determined "to concentrate only on Jesus Christ and his death on the cross" (1 Cor. 2:1, 2). The apostle had concluded that he had to deal with the basic issue facing humanity: How does God deal with the sin problem? And he wanted to find some way of impressing on the Corinthians that God did so through the death of Jesus Christ.

As we think about the topic of grace and atonement we immediately confront the gospel story of the crucifixion and death of Jesus Christ, and must face the fundamental question: Why did Christ have to die? Was there no other way to "save" the sinner? And for whose benefit did He die? Was it to appease His Father and to solve God's dilemma? Or was it for all men and women who were and are willing to rely for their eternal salvation on the divine intervention on their behalf on the cross? This then leads to the next question: What is the relationship between divine love and justice?

In our day and age many people with a postmodern worldview

find the traditional concept of atonement totally unpalatable. If human beings have made mistakes, they should be held responsible and make amends themselves. The very idea that someone else would have to accept punishment in their stead revolts them. It is a superstitious theory of the past—when people still needed some hocus-pocus to deal with their feelings of guilt. It was a concept carefully stimulated by the clergy, who were always eager to find ways of wielding their power over their ignorant parishioners. Fortunately, that is not the position of Seventh-day Adventist Christians.

The special branch of theology that deals with grace and related issues goes by the name of soteriology—the science of salvation. That term suggests that salvation is something very complicated and requires great scholarship if we are to fathom what it is about. Indeed, theologians have, through the ages, written heavy tomes to present their various theories. Some have stressed the idea of satisfaction, whereby the demands of the divine law are met and divine justice is satisfied. Others stress the forensic—that is, the legal and penal aspects, of atonement. A third category of theories highlights, in particular, the element of substitution (someone being punished in our place), while there are, finally, also theologians who see the atonement mainly, or exclusively, in terms of its moral influence. Which theories are most biblical?

Theologians have to base their theological constructs on the building blocks provided in Scripture. They also employ words that, though not appearing as such in the Bible, are believed to summarize Biblical concepts. The list of such terms is impressive. The most frequently mentioned are: salvation, reconciliation, expiation, propitiation, ransom, redemption, sacrifice, judgment and wrath, satisfaction, and substitution. However, all theological approaches fall, in fact, into two classes: subjective and objective theories.

Those who defend a subjective theory of some kind suggest that the cross was, first of all, a demonstration of God's love rather than a legal arrangement of credits and debits, with our sins being weighed against Christ's innocence. The cross, they say, so impresses us that it gives us strength and determination to change our behavior and follow Christ. We become immersed in an atmosphere of gracious self-giving. Thus the cross "happened" in order to trigger a human response of love.

But the theologians who support an objective view of the atonement disagree. They maintain that something real and concrete happened at Golgotha that makes an objective difference. God had to deal with the sin problem through a divine act. Being the source of love as well as of justice, He had to mete out a punishment in a historical event. Humanity would have to die because of its sins, but on a Friday afternoon, around the year A.D. 31, Christ died in Jerusalem as our substitute. A price had to be paid. And the price *was* paid.

Seventh-day Adventists support the objective view of atonement, although they recognize that the subjective view also has merit, and that both views do not exclude each other. Yet we must never think that we can reduce every aspect of the atonement to neat formulas. Human words cannot adequately describe the mystery of evil. Neither can they fully define the mystery of grace (Eph. 3). It is, however, important never to reduce our view of the atonement just to what happens *in* us when we contemplate the miracle of the cross that took place *for* us. Our contemplation can have effect only if something decisive happened when Christ died at the cross. It is the only way in which I can read such passages as Romans 3:23-25:

"For all have sinned; all fall short of God's glorious standard. Yet now God in his gracious kindness declares us not guilty. He has done this through Christ Jesus, who has freed us by taking away our sins. For God sent Jesus to take the punishment for our sins. . . . We are made right with God when we believe that Jesus shed his blood, sacrificing his life for us."

And 1 Peter 2:24:

"He personally carried our sins in his own body on the cross so we can be dead to sin and live for what is right. You have been healed by his wounds."

God's options

One of the central Christian doctrines is that Christ's death somehow put us right with God and has given us a fresh start. Now, imagine what God could have done with regard to the appearance of human sin. Humanly speaking, we can think of four options:

Conceivably, He could have created us in such a way that it would have been impossible for us to sin. He could have made us without a free will—as robots. But such virtues as obedience, goodness, and loving service would have been totally meaningless.

God could have executed Adam and Eve immediately after the Fall, and could have started all over again, this time making it impossible for His creatures ever to repeat their mistake. The same objections apply as in 1.

God could have abandoned His creation. If He had ignored humanity, it would soon have passed off the scene and human history would have ended, because, if left to itself, sin is totally self-destructive.

God could operate on the basis of grace and take sin upon Himself and deal with it in such a way as to vanquish it.

Some might also argue that He could have wiped the slate clean and simply ignored the fact that the human race had sinned. But that was no option. God is holy and cannot tolerate sin, because sin opposes everything that God wants and everything that He is. Sin is not merely a regrettable communication problem between God and humanity. No, it leads to a final, irrevocable break between the Creator and the creature. No human solution will work. It requires a divine remedy: grace!

When discussing atonement, we must remember that God takes the initiative in dealing with sin. "This is real love. It is not that we loved God, but that he loved us and sent his Son as a sacrifice to take away our sins" (1 John 4:10). The cross is the decisive moment in the process of divine love. Everything before prepares for this moment, and everything afterward is consequence. Salvation finds its center in the cross. But the cross was not an afterthought or a belated measure of desperate damage control. "Long ago, even before he made the world, God loved us and chose us in Christ" (Eph. 1:4). Christ is the Lamb of God, "who was killed before the world was made" (Rev. 13:8). That was the foundation for salvation history. After His death Christ continued to minister as the mediator in the heavenly sanctuary (Heb. 8:2). Only when we have inherited the new earth will the process of salvation be complete.

The reality of the cross

Today it is trendy to paint Jesus as a victim—a victim of hate and abuse, of discrimination and of human rights violation. Thereby, Jesus becomes a symbol for the millions who in the course of history have become victims of crimes against humanity: the slaves sold as cattle to work the plantations, the inmates of Auschwitz, the victims of Hiroshima, the Blacks under South African apartheid, the Indians in North America, the Aborigines in Australia, the students on the Tiananmen Square, and all those who suffered and still suffer under totalitarian regimes. All this is true enough. Jesus became the victim of human evil, His death the greatest miscarriage of judgment ever. His crucifixion was a terrible crime against basic human rights.

But the full story is not yet told when we make Him the symbol of all who have suffered injustice. The uniqueness of the story of the cross is in what lies behind the drama of Calvary. The hands of those who beat Him and vilified Him were not the most important hands in this tragedy. The depth of the story is in the holy hands of God the Father, which were stretched out over his Son. Not the hammers and nails of the Roman soldiers are the focus, but the intensity of the divine incompatibility with sin. The cross did not just happen—as something that got out of hand. The plans of the priests and Pharisees were not the decisive factor. The cross was part of "God's prearranged plan" of grace, as the apostle Peter affirmed at the day of Pentecost (Acts 2:23).

Yet, we should not see the drama as a prefixed scenario that Jesus had no choice but to subject to. He could have refused to bear the cross. But, in His love, He accepted it and went to the end, until He could say: "It is finished!" (John 19:30). When Christ died, "darkness fell across the whole land" (Matt. 27:45) as a token that something of unique importance had occurred. His final cry was not the shout of a dying man who knew His physical suffering was over, but expressed the glorious truth that He had forever accomplished His task: hell had been conquered; the salvation of the human race was a fact; the sacrifice had been brought—never to be repeated or to be improved upon. Christ's death had bridged the abyss of sin. The Lamb of God had indeed taken away the sins of the world (John 1:29)!

Images of atonement

Human words cannot adequately describe the mystery of grace. The various theories that theologians have constructed can help us only to catch a glimpse. The many different metaphors of the Bible writers all contribute to our wonder and appreciation of this unparalleled demonstration of divine compassion, but leave many questions unanswered.

Among the images used in the Bible we find a number that were inspired by Israel's sacrificial system. The New Testament describes Christ as "the sacrifice for our sins" that "takes away not only our sins but the sins of the world" (1 John 2:2). Jesus "shed his blood, sacrificing his life for us" (Rom. 3:25). Many Bible passages refer to Him as "the Lamb of God." Isaiah 53—the section about the Suffering Servant—expands on this theme in the most sublime way. It pictures Christ as "a lamb [that is led] to the slaughter" (verse 7) and that is "wounded and crushed for our sins" (verse 5). This beautiful chapter emphasizes the element of substitution. Christ steps in and takes our place before God. He gets what we deserve, while we receive what He deserves. Jesus accepts the punishments that are the result of our sins, while we inherit the privileges of his divine Sonship.

The Old Testament sacrificial system was not a clever adaptation of pagan ideas and rites, but an essential part of the divine revelation that something drastic would be needed to restore the broken relationship between God and humanity. Everything that happened in the tabernacle and the Temple was a magnificent *tableau vivant*, a vibrant object lesson of how God would deal with sin. When the reality had come and the true Lamb was slain, the illustrations had fulfilled their purpose. The curtain in the Temple between the Holy of Holies and the holy was rent asunder as a clear signal that reality had overtaken the shadow.

Here we encounter in an unfathomable way the miracle of

God's grace. God's mercy did not reveal itself in a weakness that simply ignores. Nor did it lose itself in a sentimentality that surreptitiously dropped the demands of God's holy law. Here we meet all-consuming love. Love that cost God dearly. Love that required the life of His own Son. More He could not give. When a sinless Being enters this world, people put Him to death. That is what sinful humanity does. But there is also another side to it. For when a sinless Being enters this world, He dies to save the world. That is what God does.

Scripture takes other images about salvation from the world of law and economics. We must realize that they are metaphors and must not apply them beyond what they try to express. But they leave a vivid impression on our minds. Take Mark 10:45 as an example: "I, the Son of Man, came here not to be served but to serve others, and to give my life as a ransom for many." The idea of a ransom—the payment of a price by a redeemer—is a well-known Old Testament concept, and it should not surprise us that the New Testament writers were inspired to use it: "There is only one God and one Mediator who can reconcile God and people. He is the man Christ Jesus. He gave his life to purchase freedom for everyone" (1 Tim. 2:5, 6). No longer is humanity the property of the evil one—God has brought us back into His family. He has bought us for a "high price" (1 Cor. 6:20). "God paid a ransom to save [us] from the empty life [that we] inherited from [our] ancestors. And the ransom he paid was not mere gold or silver. . . . [It was] the precious lifeblood of Christ, the sinless, spotless Lamb of God" (1 Peter 1:18, 19).

Another category of images may not appeal as much to us as it might have done to our first-century brothers and sisters, who first read the portion of Scriptures that employed metaphors of war and victory. Golgotha is the place of cosmic victory. The "evil rulers and authorities of the unseen world, . . . those mighty powers of darkness, . . . and . . . wicked spirits in the heavenly realms" (Eph. 6:12) are word pictures of the evil influences around us that seduce us, try to destroy us, and do all they can to distance us from the only true Lord. The joyful message of the New Testament is that *Christus*

Victor has dethroned all such influences and powers. He "disarmed the evil rulers and authorities. He shamed them publicly by his victory over them on the cross" (Col. 2:15). Yes, these powers still exist, but they are mere phantoms that no longer have the last word. God has conquered them—forever.

Our response

We now come full circle. Something of unprecedented proportions took place almost 2,000 years ago. It was a concrete, objective, historical, and suprahistorical fact. Of course, the question remains relevant what this means to us. Many around us are virtually unaware of the fact of the atonement. And for many others, who know the story full well, it makes very little difference to their daily life. It reminds us of the words of Peter, who predicted that there will be "scoffers who will laugh at the truth" and who will say: "As far back as anyone can remember, everything has remained exactly the same since the world was first created" (2 Peter 3:4). Such "scoffers" are, however, totally mistaken, for everything has changed. The balance of power in the universe has shifted once and for all. When Christ was dying on the cross, He did not say "It is almost finished!" or "One day it will be finished!" *No—He said, "It is finished!"*

Nonetheless, what Jesus achieved at Calvary must be implemented. Christ ministers in the heavenly sanctuary to ensure that we can reap eternal benefit from what He accomplished. While Christ is our great high priest, mediating for us on the basis of what He achieved, we are patiently but eagerly expecting the moment that He will come to make all things new. In the interim He calls us to be His disciples, to rally behind Him and carry the cross that will be laid on us. For now we must learn to live by the law of faith, and must continue to grow in grace. We live in the assurance of salvation. "For his Holy Spirit speaks to us deep in our hearts and tells us that we are God's children" (Rom. 8:17). Being assured of salvation and of His generous forgiveness, we will do all that we can to live worthy of that privilege. "Should we keep on sinning so that God can show us more and more kindness and forgiveness?" (Rom.

6:1). The answer is self-evident: "Of course not! Since we have died to sin, how can we continue to live in it?" (verse 2). Having been saved, we want to live as Christ's disciples, being guided by the principles of the kingdom.

At this point it is good to quote extensively from 2 Corinthians 5. Verses 18-21 point to what comes next. If we are reconciled (atoned, or "made at one"), we want others to have the same experience:

"All this newness of life is from God, who brought us back to himself through what Christ did. And God has given us the task of reconciling people to him. For God was in Christ, reconciling the world to himself, no longer counting people's sins against them. This is the wonderful message he has given us to tell others. We are Christ's ambassadors, and God is using us to speak to you. We urge you, as though Christ himself were here pleading with you, 'Be reconciled to God!' For God made Christ, who never sinned, to be the offering for our sin, so that we could be made right with God through Christ."

We are reconciled. We are saved. But we will never fully understand what this means. To many the idea of "Christ . . . crucified" (1 Cor. 1:23) remains "a stumblingblock" (verse 23, KJV) or utter "nonsense" (verse 23). Many who profess to be Christians are stuck in their misconception that the atonement is something an angry deity demands, and miss the glorious truth that it is something a God of love and grace provides!

REST 8

"While our speed may keep us safe, it also keeps us malnour-
ished. It prevents us from tasting those things that would truly
make us safe. Prayer, touch, kindness, fragrance—all those
things that live in rest, and not in speed."

—WAYNE MULLER,
Sabbath, p. 53

When God created our world, He also inaugurated time as we
know it. For us humans, the movement of heavenly bodies
regulates time. The turning of the earth around its axis determines
the length of the day. The month depends on the relative
movements of earth and moon, while the movement of the earth
relative to the sun gives us the year. Later we humans were clever
enough to come up with smaller units of time: hours, quarter hours,
minutes, seconds. More recently science has introduced the concept
of nanoseconds (one billionth of a second). But when "God created
heaven and earth," He also established another unit of time, one not
related to any movement of either our planet or of the moon or
sun—the seven-day week.

For those who do not believe in the Creation narrative, the origin of the week will remain an insolvable mystery. Scholars have
done a lot of research and speculation. It has been suggested that
some ancient peoples had market days, and that somewhere one society held its market day once every seven days and that this was the
murky origin of our week. Others have propounded additional theories, but they have no solid evidence to work with. As a result, the
origin of the week and of the weekly day of rest must remain a mys-

tery, unless you are prepared to believe in the biblical Creation story.

The Creation story suggests that the seven-day week is a fundamental arrangement. You cannot get rid of it, however much you would try. At the time of their revolution in July 1789 the French sought to replace the traditional week with a 10-day cycle. It did not work out as the revolutionary leaders had expected, and the government abolished the experiment only a few years later. Through the centuries humanity has made other attempts to modify the weekly cycle. I remember how in the 1960s Adventist periodicals printed many articles about a proposed calendar reform that would result in the insertion of blank days, and, as result, would greatly upset the regular Sabbath cycle. The commotion about this particular campaign died down after some time and was soon forgotten. A bit of Googling on the Internet, however, reveals that the idea of reforming the calendar, though not as drastically as in the time of the French Revolution, stills keeps plenty of minds occupied. It seems fair to predict however that the divine invention of the week is stronger than the human attempts to dabble with it.

The Creation story informs us about not only the origin of the week but also the institution of the weekly Sabbath on day seven. When God saw that what He had created "was good," He "rested" from creating—that is, He stopped creating and gave that seventh day a special meaning. He made it "holy" by setting it apart. It would be an honored day. And thus He instituted the unique rhythm of six plus one that has governed the flow of time ever since. This is the pulse of life on Planet Earth for as long as humanity will live here—and even on the new world that will eventually replace it.

Thank God for the Sabbath

Today we find more interest in the phenomenon of the Sabbath than has existed for quite a long time. Many books have appeared in recent years extolling the virtues of keeping the Sabbath. It is not difficult to see why there is such a renewed interest in a regular day of rest. We talk a lot about time management. We have so much to do, and time is usually in painfully short supply. How do we use our time more efficiently? How can we reduce the amount that we waste? How do we prioritize and spend quality time on what is most important? How do we learn to work methodically and delegate wherever possible? And where on earth do we find regular time to relax?

Many heralded the introduction of the computer as the beginning of a new era, in which we would hardly need paper anymore, and in which the length of our workweek would drastically shrink. Both predictions have failed utterly and miserably. It seems that we consume more, rather than less, paper with our ever more sophisticated printers and copiers on ever more preliminary drafts of ever longer documents. And it is likely that the number of hours we have to work will actually increase to more than 40 hours per week, rather than descend below 30, as many believed it would.

There is a strange anomaly in the way we experience our time. On the one hand, we see something that we might call "the worship of the weekend." I am no longer amazed when people start wishing me a good weekend from Thursday afternoon onward. Yes, for many the weekend is the oasis in time for which they live. When Monday starts, it is just a few days until the next weekend comes around again. But then we have so much to do in the weekend. Even what is supposed to be recreation often takes on such a serious form that it begins to feel like hard work. And also, for many of us the concerns of work accompany us when we shut our office door for the duration of the weekend. We still have so much to read, so many reports to write, calls to make, e-mails to respond to. Most of us who work at middle management level, or above, know how vague the borderlines have often become between work time and free time. The other day I read somewhere about a man who came back from his vacation. "Ready for work again," he announced as he transferred his laptop from his backpack to his attaché case!

The Western world seems to be hit by an epidemic of heart infarcts, burnouts, high blood pressure, and life-threatening stress. Our doctors tell us that we must learn to slow down if we want to survive. We must cure ourselves of our infection with the deadly virus of workaholism. Once again we must learn to listen to the inbuilt rhythm of our bodies. In other words, we must rediscover true rest as a regular feature of our physical and spiritual existence.

Adventists have a message for the people around them that has a direct connection with this. It is is not new, yet, it is "present truth." The message is that the rest that we need is available. The weekly Sabbath is the perfect antidote for a life in which work and social duty hold us hostage, seemingly with no way of escape. The Sabbath reminds us that work and duty have their rightful place. As a result of sin, work may have acquired negative aspects, admittedly for some more than for others. The tendency toward workaholism and the danger of becoming slaves of what we do may well be a contemporary form of the curse linked to work after Adam's fall (Gen. 3:18). The Sabbath is the medicine that exceeds all attractively packaged placebos of amusement and recreation. It enables us to put our work truly behind us. And it reminds us that, important though our work may be, true life has more to it than career and money. There is a way of really getting away from it for a full 24 hours. God provides a marvelous method of escape through the Sabbath.

Rest

The Sabbath is the day of rest. That certainly includes physical rest. It is great to be able to unwind on Friday evening and to get up a bit later on Sabbath morning. I have long ago stopped feeling guilty when I take a nap on Sabbath afternoon. But "rest" in the biblical sense is much more than a bit of sleep. The classical text about the rest that the believer can enjoy is, of course, Matthew 11:28, 29: "Come to me, all of you who are weary and carry heavy burdens, and *I will give you rest*. Take my yoke upon you. Let me teach you, because I am humble and gentle, and *you will find rest* for your souls." Genuine rest is not just the result of stretching out on the couch or relaxing in the garden or on the balcony. The deep rest that we need is of divine origin. The "master . . . of the Sabbath" (Mark 2:28) provides that rest at all times, but in particular on His day of rest.

In the book of Hebrews this concept of rest is very prominent. God wanted His people of old to experience His "rest" upon entering the Promised Land. Finding this rest would involve not ever having to work again. It meant that a deep sense of satisfaction and fulfillment, a precious experience of peace and closeness to their God, would forever characterize their lives. Things did, however, not work out as God had planned. The people of Israel did not "enter" such rest in the measure that God had intended for them. Their lack of commitment to Him kept them away from the promised rest. But God never gives up. "There is a special rest still waiting for the people of God" (Heb. 4:9). Such rest in its fullness awaits God's people in the hereafter. But, very significantly, we find a number of links in the fourth chapter of the book of Hebrews between this eternal "rest" and the weekly Sabbath in our present world. The very word *sabbatismos* used for this rest in verse 9 clearly reminds us of its connection with the seventh day. The seventh day of each week presents us with a preview and foretaste of this heavenly rest that is as yet future.

Remember by keeping it *holy*

The Sabbath commandment as recorded in Exodus 20 begins with a word pregnant with meaning: *Remember*. For us, remembering is first of all a function of part of our brain. We must remember lots of things, and sometimes fail deplorably in keeping in mind important things. Some of us have a better memory than others. In the Bible the words translated as "remembering" do not, however, primarily refer to a function of the right lobe of our brain. When God assures us that He "remembers" us, or when we ask Him to "remember" us, it does not mean that God may temporarily have lost sight of us and needs to be reminded of the fact that we are still there and still need Him. His remembering refers to his active involvement in love and compassion. Israel, in Old Testament times, was constantly urged to remember what the Lord God had done for them. The annual feasts had this primary function: to pause and consider—individually, as a family and as a community—how God in His compassionate love had guided and saved them. The Christian believers were to celebrate the Lord's Supper on a regular basis "in remembrance" of what Christ had done (Luke 22:19). Here, again, Scripture does not use the element of "remembering" accidentally. It still has the same intense significance. We do not take part in the Communion service just because it happens to be an ancient tradition that we must not forget. No, we are fully immersed in the experience. We are in touch in a very real way with God's love and compassion.

The fact that God instructs us to remember the Sabbath does, admittedly, also have the meaning of returning to something that we may have forgotten. That was true of the Israelites in the desert, whom God reminded of the importance of the weekly Sabbath when the manna failed to appear on the seventh day. Apparently God's people had largely forgotten Sabbath observance, and He needed to alert them to the fact that the commandment had not been abolished. That may be the case for us, or for some of our families. But "remembering" the Sabbath involves more. It is, first and foremost, opening ourselves up to the reality of God's love and compassion for His creatures.

We remember by keeping the day holy. The experience of the reality of God's compassionate love for us is facilitated by the way we approach the Sabbath day. Keeping it "holy" means setting it apart, making it special. People and objects that had a specialized function in Old Testament worship were said to be "holy." They were singled out for special use and not available for profane purposes. God's people in New Testament times are also spoken of as holy. They are certainly not holy in the sense of being sinless or perfect. But they are holy, because of the role in God's plan of salvation that He set them apart for. Later we will return in a little more detail to what keeping the day holy may imply for Christians in the twenty-first century.

A symbol of obedience

Several of the books about the Sabbath that have recently appeared contain some enlightening statements about the meaning of the Sabbath. Even the current pope has surprised many of us in his recent book about the person and work of Christ with his insightful remarks about the biblical meaning of the Sabbath and about what it means to recognize Christ as the Lord of the Sabbath.[1] But, almost without exception, these books simply ignore a crucial aspect of the Sabbath. As a rule they just assume that there is no problem whatsoever in taking the liberty to shift all that is said about the Sabbath to Sunday. Usually a short comment will suffice to take care of the situation—Sunday, we are told, gradually replaced the Sabbath, and the church saw no problem in accepting this transfer and in adopting Sunday as the weekly day of rest. After all, it is usually added, the first day of the week is the day of the Resurrection and it is only fitting that Christians pay special attention to that day. Most people who become aware of this human-made shift from the seventh to the first day of the week do not see that it matters very much. As long as we "keep" one day in seven, they say, it does not make much difference which day it is.

Seventh-day Adventists strongly disagree. Sunday and Sabbath are not interchangeable, whatever people may think. God is particular. If He decides to "bless" a particular day and to "declare it holy" (see Gen. 2:3), who are we to question His judgment and to declare the issue unimportant? Could God have been more explicit when He gave the wording of the Sabbath commandment to Moses: "The *seventh day* is a day of rest dedicated to the Lord your God. . . . For in six days the Lord made the heavens, the earth, the sea, and everything in them; then he rested *on the seventh day*. That is why the Lord blessed the Sabbath day and set it apart as holy" (Ex. 20:10, 11)?

It is actually all quite straightforward. Celebrating the Sabbath on the seventh day of the week is part of the Ten Commandments, the divine constitution for humanity. These commandments retain their validity as long as this world exists. Christ did not come to abolish them, as some Christians have mistakenly suggested. Instead He assures us: "Until heaven and earth disappear, even the smallest detail of God's law will remain" (Matt. 5:18). We are not to be selective about what commandments we choose to obey and which ones we choose to alter or neglect. "And the person who keeps all of the laws except one is as guilty as a person who has broken all of God's laws" (James 2:10). Those who want to belong to God's people will "remain firm to the end, *obeying his commands* and trusting in Jesus" (Rev. 14:12).

An important aspect of the Advent message is communicating in all possible ways the proclamation of the first angel: "Worship him who made heaven and earth" (verse 7). Even many who profess to believe in Him have discredited the truth of God as Creator. By keeping the Sabbath on the seventh day of the week, God's people continue to emphasize His creatorship and all that it entails. This, Adventists believe, adds tremendously to the special significance of the Sabbath for today. Therefore they do not hesitate to refer to the Sabbath as God's *seal* of ownership. The Sabbath proclaims that God "owns" His people. He created them and redeemed them. As in Old Testament times, when the Sabbath was a permanent sign of God's covenant (Ex. 31:13, 17; Eze. 20:12, 20), so in "the time of the end" the Sabbath is a "sign" of allegiance to God the Creator. Adventist Christians feel privileged and are proud to be marked with that sign of loyalty. It may at times be socially inexpedient; and it may at some future time cause major trouble if one persists in not going with the tide, but they want to belong to the "remnant"— those who have resolved not to follow human tradition. They know that it is all worth it. After all, He has attached His blessing to this day. Only by showing our allegiance to Him, and being obedient to what He asks, can we hope to enjoy the fullness of that blessing!

Again: keeping the seventh day "holy"

It is important that we know *when* to keep the Sabbath. But it is just as important to know *how* to celebrate this special day that God has set apart. I use *celebrate* for good reason. Christians have indeed much to celebrate. God created us, and we are, therefore, His creatures who are privileged to bear His image. But, as followers of Christ, we know also that we are redeemed. The version of the Ten Commandments in Deuteronomy 5 emphasizes this aspect. God said to Israel: "Remember that you were once slaves in Egypt and that the Lord your God brought you out with amazing power and mighty deeds" (verse 15). Whatever form our Egypt may have, the words are directed as much to us as to the Israelites. The Ten Commandments remind us that we are twice His—by creation and by redemption! So, yes, there is every reason for celebration.

But, *in concreto*, how do we celebrate? How do we keep the Sabbath holy? How do we "enjoy" the day of the Lord and "speak of it with delight" (Isa. 58:13)? Many of us must admit that we have not always been successful in this respect. Some second- and third-generation Adventists, thinking of the many do's and don'ts surrounding the observance of the Sabbath in their parental home, do not always remember the Sabbath days of their youth as pure delight, and many Adventist college students unfortunately do not feel that they hugely "enjoy" the Sabbath.

The remainder of the text we just quoted from Isaiah has also resulted in plenty of feelings of guilt. After having told his audience that the Sabbath is meant to be a delight, the prophet tells the people that on the seventh day we are not to follow our "own desires or talk idly" (verse 13). What does this mean? Does that force us in an ill-fitting straitjacket that hardly gives us room to breathe?

We are aware of some other Old Testament passages that fill us with fear rather than delight. What do we do with a story such as, for instance, that in Numbers 15, in which we read how someone caught an Israelite red-handed collecting fire wood on a Sabbath and had him brought to Moses and Aaron, who decided that the man was to be punished? As a result the community stoned him to death (verses 32-36). What do we make of this?

In general, we must conclude that we know very little about how people observed the Sabbath through the centuries. Often they did not keep it at all. At times, the Old Testament prophets issued stern warnings against an empty, ritualistic approach to the Sabbath, which they denounced as "sinful and false" (Isa. 1:13). We know that by the time of Christ Sabbath observance had for many become extremely legalistic, with a long list of categories of work forbidden on it. The implications were often almost bizarre. When Christ went on a Sabbath walk together with His disciples, they picked up a few heads of wheat, rubbed them in their hands, and ate a few grains. Jesus' critics immediately classified it as "harvesting," one of the categories of work strictly forbidden on the Sabbath (Luke 6:1-5). From all we read in the New Testament it is clear that Jesus' approach to the Sabbath was very different from that of most of the spiritual leaders. That is, for instance, visible in the many healings He performed on the Sabbath. He left no doubt that He had no intention of abolishing the divine law. Rather He emphasized its deeper intention. The commandments concern not just our external action, but also our innermost motives (see Matt. 5:21-48). Most important, He taught His disciples that the Sabbath is primarily about building a relationship with Him, who is "master even of the Sabbath" (Mark 2:28).

Nonetheless, we still face the practical question of *How?* How exactly do we "remember" the Sabbath by keeping it "holy"? I have traveled widely in many parts of the world and have found that Adventists differ greatly in the ways in which they attempt to do this. Things considered in some countries as absolutely unsuitable for the Sabbath hours Adventists in other parts of the world regard as quite acceptable. Some forms of Sabbath recreation are frowned upon in some places, but are part of the regular pattern of Sabbath keeping in other areas. In some regions the issue of whether or not one has to pay money to engage in a certain activity is the determining factor, while elsewhere church members do not see it as very important. A few years ago May-Ellen Colon, a departmental assistant director at the General Conference, wrote her doctoral dissertation on this topic.[2] Her study provides a solid academic confirmation of what I and many others have experienced while traveling around the globe. What do we conclude? Is everything acceptable as long as we feel good about it? Or should we send some severe warning messages to other areas of the world to tell our spiritual sisters and brothers that they should desist from their errors and rather do as we do? Let me, in closing this chapter, make a few suggestions.

1. Keeping "holy" or "setting apart" is not something that happens by accident. It demands intentional and continuous effort. Frequently some have used the metaphor of a "hedge" that we should place around the Sabbath—keeping certain things in and other things out.

2. The Bible is our guide to discover the basic principles of Sabbath observance, and we believe we have further guidance from the writings of Ellen White. We must take care to identify the underlying principles and apply them to our twenty-first-century situation. (Just a simple example: When the commandment tells me not to "covet" my neighbor's donkey, I immediately sense that it may have something to do about me and my neighbor's Porsche or BMW.)

3. What we keep within the "hedge" or shut out, depends to

some extent on our history and culture. (Because I live in a country that once was predominantly Calvinistic, my Sabbath observance has probably always shown some similarities with the way in which many orthodox Protestants around me used to keep their Sunday.)

4. The community of which we are part plays a role in determining where we will place the hedge. That is not to say that we should not exercise personal choice, but being part of a community inevitably influences us.

5. The things I choose to do on Sabbath, or decide to exclude, may differ from what someone else may select to include or exclude. (With a hundred or so e-mails on many workdays, I may want to keep the lid of my laptop firmly closed on Sabbath, while others may decide it is the best day to get in touch with friends and relatives.)

6. Beware of two extremes: (a) legalism and (b) carelessness. Both will destroy the blessing of the Sabbath.

7. It all boils down to making sure that we fill the Sabbath with good things: worship, fellowship, family, friends. If those things get priority, most other things fall into their rightful place.

8. And, when others do not quite follow the same pattern you do, decide not to be judgmental. They may be right; you may be wrong.

9. Finally, allow for growth. You may, over the years, have grown and matured in your way of keeping the Sabbath holy. Give others the time and space for that same process of growth.

When all is said and done, it is crucial to take the spirit of the Sabbath with you during the other days of the week. The spirit of worship and the new attitude toward our daily work that the Sabbath fosters can bring a great blessing that can spill over into every hour of the week.

---

[1] Pope Benedict XVI, *Jesus of Nazareth* (Random House, 2007).

[2] May-Ellen Colon, *Sabbathkeeping Practices and Factors Related to These Practices Among Seventh-day Adventists in 51 Countries* (Ph.D. diss., Andrews University, 2003).

HEAVEN 9

"There is a land of pure delight,
Where saints immortal reign;
Infinite day excludes the night,
And pleasures banish pain.

"There everlasting spring abides,
And never-withering flowers;
And but a little space divides
This heavenly land from ours."

—ISAAC WATTS

During three rather controversial Wednesday audiences in 1999, Pope John Paul II stated that we should not interpret heaven, hell, or purgatory as places, but rather as states of being of a spirit (angel or demon) or a human soul. The statement contains a number of theological errors, but here we are mainly concerned with the assertion that heaven is not a place but a condition. The language of place is, according to the pope, inadequate to describe the realities involved, since it is tied to the temporal order in which this world and we exist. He added that his view has long been a venerable position, one also defended by the famous Thomas Aquinas. Is this view of heaven biblically sound? Many theologians would say yes. Most Adventists would say no. Which perspective is correct? Here we have but one of several burning questions that we must face as we grapple with the concept of heaven.

Where is heaven?

I suggest that you find an encyclopedia—either in the library or in digital form—and take a look at the entry entitled "Heaven." You will find the word used in many different ways. It may refer to the visible sky, or the the endless expanse of the physical universe. But people also employ it to describe the location, or the condition, to which we may go after death, as disembodied souls or as beings with a new spiritual body. If you consult a concordance and check on Bible texts in which the words "heaven," "heavens," and "heavenly" occur, you will also find that the words have different connotations in Scripture. God created the heavens and the earth. He set the lights of sun, moon, and stars "in the heavens to light the earth" (Gen. 1:17). But the terms do not refer to the firmament only, but also to the realm of God and angels. God is said to "live" in "heaven" (Rev. 13:6). In addition, Scripture can employ "heaven" as a synonym for God, as for instance in the phrase "the kingdom of heaven."

One might ask how we could say that God "lives" in *one* place called "heaven," while one of the attributes of God is His omnipresence. He is not to be identified with everything that exists, such as pantheists claim, but He is always present everywhere (see Ps. 139:7-12). So how can we reconcile the concept of omnipresence with the idea that He lives in a specific place? God, the Gospel of John tells us, "is Spirit" (John 4:24). What does that mean? At the very least, it implies that we should not think of Him as a being with a material body such as we have, "living" in a material place in the same way that we do. "He lives in light so brilliant that no human can approach him" (1 Tim. 6:16).

The concept of "heaven" gets expressed in many different ways—not only in theology, but also in artwork, narrative, poetry, liturgy, and folklore. Just how people have conceptualized heaven has always greatly differed.[1] In the Old Testament the contours of heaven, as the place for a life after death, remain rather sketchy. During the time of Christ the spiritual leaders had a divided opinion. The Sadducees did not believe in a life in a heavenly hereafter (Matt. 22:23ff.), whereas the Pharisees did. At this point Jesus clearly sided with the Pharisees, as we understand from the way in which He replied to the trick question of the Sadducees. They were curious, they said, what would happen when a man had been married seven times in this life. Jesus answered that the problem as to who would belong to whom in the hereafter would not pose itself, as those who inherit eternity "won't be married. They will be like the angels in heaven" (Matt. 22:23-30). Paul struggles to find the words that will adequately explain his visionary experience on the Damascus road. He states: "I was caught up into the third heaven" (2 Cor. 12:2). Elsewhere in his letters he speaks of the hereafter where the saved live in spiritual bodies, freed from all physical restraints. The book of Hebrews speaks of heaven as God's residence, where we find the heavenly tabernacle and where Christ ministers as our high priest. The book of Revelation presents us with vivid descriptions of the divine throne room and the exuberant worship services that take place in heaven. It ends by singing the praises of the new heavens and the new earth, in which God and His people will eventually enjoy each other's eternal company.

As the centuries roll by, we see how each epoch paints its own picture of what it expects heaven to be like. The images fluctuate from very materialistic descriptions to utterly ascetic images. At times the emphasis is on the future Paradise as an Edenic garden that provides the perfect setting for the supreme enjoyment of beauty and love, and for an incessant contemplation of the divine in what has often been referred to as the beatific vision. But looking at many medieval paintings of heaven, we see how in the Middle Ages the growth of the cities in ancient Europe led increasingly to a portrayal of heaven in more urban terms. The descriptions of the Protestant Reformers seem to center more on God Himself than on His heavenly environment. The Reformers do not spend much time debating what heaven is like, but often sharply differ on how we get there. Catholics emphasize also the role of Mary and the saints, who, they say, have preceded us to heaven and intercede for us. In more recent Protestantism the concern of meeting family and loved ones who have left us plays a crucial role.

Today, many Christians think as Pope John Paul II did. They consider the view that heaven is a real place as crude, or at very best naive. Liberal theologians have at times proposed theories based on the concept of "realized" eschatology. By this they mean that the things most Christians have traditionally seen as in the future (when the "time of the end" would come, and when Christ would return to create a new world) will already be realized in the here and now. They have done away with the idea of a future kingdom of God, and take the text in which Christ says that "the Kingdom of God isn't ushered in with visible signs. . . . For the Kingdom of God is among you" (Luke 17:20, 21) as their point of departure. But more conservative circles, such as the Adventist Church, still look upon heaven as a concrete place—whatever difficulties that admittedly may imply.

Early Adventists tended to describe heaven in more materialistic terms than most Adventists do today. The gradual shift toward stressing human inability to imagine and to describe the heavenly realm is even visible in the writings of Ellen G. White. She received her first vision in 1844, shortly after the Disappointment. Published a year later in *The Day-Star,* one of the early Adventist periodicals, it makes fascinating reading. Ellen White "was shown something of the travels of the Advent people to the Holy City." It took seven days to ascend to the "sea of glass." As she entered the New Jerusalem, she saw harps of gold and palms of victory given to travelers. She also viewed the tree of life and the throne of God. Most telling is perhaps the comment that she was able to speak with men named Fitch and Stockman, who had been active leaders in the Advent movement.[2]

Some statements made by Ellen White may surprise us in their detailed description of aspects of heaven. She informs us that a group of angels has been working hard through the centuries to construct the crowns that the redeemed will wear.[3] Also she assures that our heavenly "mansions" will be quite large and commodious, so that they will be suitable when those who are saved will eventually grow to the ideal stature of humanity, such as Adam once had.[4] Not only will they attain a greater height, but they will also receive wings![5] In later writings Ellen White seems to be somewhat less specific in her descriptions. But she continues to affirm that we should not be so fearful of making the future inheritance seem too material, that we "spiritualize away the very truths which lead us to look upon it as our home." Yet, we must also recognize, she adds, that "human language is inadequate to describe the reward of the righteous. It will be known only to those who behold it. No finite mind can comprehend the glory of the Paradise of God."[6]

When do we go to heaven?

It has been a long-cherished belief among Christians that human beings consist of a material body and a nonmaterial soul. At death the soul either goes to hell (in many cases, according to Catholic teachings, via purgatory) or to heaven. Those souls that have gone to heaven live in the presence of God while they await the future resurrection. Not only is this a very unsatisfactory explanation (for what need is there of a new material body if the soul is already perfectly happy?), but it is also unbiblical. When people die, they are reduced to dust. In a way, we may compare the state of death to sleep. The Bible actually uses the word in various places. When people die, they "lie down and do not rise again. . . . Until the heavens are no more, they will not wake up nor be roused from their sleep" (Job 14:11, 12). As death comes at our door we "will rest, and then at the end of the days, [we] will rise again to receive the inheritance set aside for [us]" (Dan. 12:13).

The resurrection of those who have chosen to be on God's side and to trust in His grace takes place when Jesus returns to the present world. It is at this point that we leave this earth and go to a destination we call heaven. Whatever it is, it includes a spatial dimension, something also implied in what Paul tries to communicate. "With the trumpet call of God" "all the Christians who have died will rise from their graves," and together with the true believers who live to experience the Second Coming, they "will be caught up in the clouds to meet the Lord in the air and remain with him forever" (1 Thess. 4:16, 17). Revelation 20 provides an important piece of information about what happens next. For "a thousand years" all those who are saved will "reign with Christ" (see verse 4) in heaven.

Christians usually refer to the period of 1,000 years as the millennium, even though the word does not appear in the Bible. It is astonishing to see how much is said and written about this 1,000-year period—though in the United States much more than in Europe and elsewhere in the Christian world. One historian, observing the spread of revivalistic millennialism, comments that nineteenth-century America was "drunk on the millennium."[7] Bible students have a number of different theories about the millennium. Amillennialism—first proposed by church father Augustine—sees the current epoch of church history, between the first and the second advent of Christ, as the millennium. Postmillennialism expects a 1,000-year period of peace (although the time period may be symbolic) preceding the second coming of Christ. Seventh-day Adventists are among those who defend premillennialism—that Christ will come, and then the millennium starts. Adventists differ sharply, however, from many evangelicals in not accepting the so-called rapture as part of the scenario that precedes the Second Coming. Taking chapter 20 of the book of Revelation as it reads, we must conclude that during the millennium the earth has become empty. Now resurrected, the "saints" have gone to heaven. Those who have rejected God will be resurrected at the end of the 1,000 years. Then, Scripture tells us, the heavenly Jerusalem with the saints will "descend" to Planet Earth. A final confrontation between the forces of evil and good will take place. It will lead to the eradication of everything that opposes God, and "a new heaven and a new earth" will now be the abode of God's children. Do you understand everything? I don't, and I do not have to. The thing that matters is crystal clear. A glorious future awaits us. We will spend time in "heaven" and then live eternally in some glorified new dimension on the earth made new!

What will it be like?

In every day and age people have tried to picture the new reality that God will create when He has finally eradicated sin. The images that we paint—whether on canvas and in prose or poetry—will always, at least to some extent, reflect the present world in which we live. When the prophet Isaiah was inspired to write about the new heavens and the new earth, he used the images he had in his creative arsenal that his audience could understand. The new heavens and the new earth that God was going to create, he said, would be a land of plenty without any poverty (see Isa. 65 and 66). No longer will people build houses for others, but they will actually live themselves in the structures they have designed and constructed and "will eat the fruit of their own vineyards" (Isa. 65:21). Death and misery will be on their way out. Dying at age 100 will be considered a premature death. Nature will be reborn, for "the wolf and the lamb will feed together" (verse 65). The lion will have become a vegetarian, and poisonous snakes will have lost their capacity of hurting anyone with their venom. "Peace and prosperity will overflow Jerusalem like a river. . . . The wealth of the nations will flow to her" (Isa. 66:12). And so Isaiah goes on! We now realize that the prophet's understanding was still limited, and that God would provide a fuller revelation. The prophet did not yet understand, as we do now, that the Messiah would not come once, to issue in better times, but that a First Advent would precede a Second Advent, and that there would be much greater discontinuity between this world and the next than God had seen fit to reveal to the Old Testament prophets. When John the revelator writes about the new heaven and the new earth, he utilizes some of the same images and adds others that were more reflective of his own days.

Even inspired writers find themselves limited when they sit down to put in words what God has revealed to them. And it is the more so the case as uninspired people try to imagine the future reality. Not surprisingly, medieval paintings of the new earth differ significantly from the illustrations by Adventist artists of the previous century, such as Harry Anderson. When I try to form some mental picture of what I may expect in the hereafter, I tend to think of the beach near the West African city of Abidjan. When I lived there during the mid-1980s and early-1990s, a stretch of tropical beach some 10 miles south of the city was our favorite spot for most of the Sunday. In my memory this weekly experience lives on as something that comes closest to how life in "paradise" might be! We all, it seems, base even our imagination on our experience of the world that we know.

But is everything that we can say about this new world that God is going to create for His people, and where He Himself will "live," no more than an extrapolation of the good things we know today? Is there nothing more that we can discover about the new creation than that it will exceed even the best things we can imagine today? It seemed that way to the apostle Paul: "No eye has seen, no ear has heard, and no mind has imagined what God has prepared for those who love him" (1 Cor. 2:9).

One might well ask how important it is to know in great detail about what will be coming. It may be that some people are perfectly happy with abstract concepts, while others long for more concrete images. But whatever be the case, we must never think that we can have a final picture as long as we live in this world, and as a result we will need to be satisfied with the limited perceptions that our senses allow for, and with the finite concepts our human brains can deal with. Questions will remain. Some of us may be more worried about these than others. As a child I wondered whether my younger brother, who died when he was only 8, would be raised as a young boy, and whether my paternal grandfather, who died a few years later at age 70, would be raised as a septuagenarian. Some may be quite happy about Jesus's remarks concerning marriage in the future life that seem to indicate that sex will forever be a thing of the past. But others will deeply worry about this statement and fear that something essential will be missing. Personally, when I read about streets of gold in a city that stretches for some 1,400 miles and has walls 216 feet thick (Rev. 21:17), I am not so sure whether that is the world of my dreams. Frankly, a cottage along some quiet country road would appeal more to me than this urban vista. There may be some who will wonder whether vacation is forever a thing of history. What a shame, they think, that there will be no sun and no more sea (Rev. 21:1; 22:5). A British Anglican bishop recently wrote a book in which he suggested that the constant worship and praise offered to God, which figure so prominently in John's descriptions of heaven, are not very attractive to many people today. Playing their harps and participating in a mass choir practice are not their preferred ways of spending time. They also wonder, he says, what kind of being we are dealing with if God is eager to have everybody, continuously and forever, sing His praises.[8]

How much of what we read in such chapters as Revelation 21 and 22 should we take in its literal sense? How much of it is symbolic? It would require more space than we have in this chapter to provide a full answer. But a few remarks will, hopefully, be helpful. The entire book of Revelation has a highly symbolic content, and it stands to reason to expect that this will therefore also apply to the last two chapters. Let us take a specific example. The book consistently uses "Babylon" symbolically. It is a comprehensive label for all powers—religious and political—that oppose God and the true worship of Him. In the prophecies of the last Bible book the name "Babylon" does not refer to a literal city, but is clearly a powerful symbol for the enemies of God. It would be consistent to conclude that the term *new Jerusalem* does not denote a literal city either, but rather is a fitting symbol for all those who will eternally be with God. If we take that approach, we can also make some sense of the description of this heavenly city. It is an immense cube, with thick walls and a dozen gates. Of course, in John's days people would think of walls and gates when picturing a city—just as we would now think of sky scrapers, highways, and other important pieces of urban infrastructure. The fact that this "city" is a cube immediately reminds us of the holiest section of the Old Testament tabernacle, which also was a perfect cube. There God was present among His people in a very special way. No wonder, then, that the idea of a cube emerges when Scripture describes a "city" in which God will be more directly present among His people than He has ever been.

So, yes, much of the language is symbolic. But symbols point to something very real. It is just that human limitations make it impossible to speak about this reality in a more direct and propositional manner. In spite of all the questions and uncertainties that remain, the final two chapters of the Bible do say enough for us to get excited about the very real future that God has in store for the redeemed.[9] We may summarize the main points as follows:

1. A total eradication of sin will characterize eternal life, heaven, and the new earth. Total love now governs all relationships.

2. Death and decay will be things of the past. With all traces of sin removed from the environment, all consequences of sin are reversed and God's reign is now realized without any imperfection or distortion.

3. As a result, eternal life will have nothing that could cause pain and fear. The new world will be so close to its source of light, that

everything bathes in this glory and all dark shadows have forever receded into oblivion.

4. In eternity God's creatures will enjoy perfect relationships. We need not worry whether, or how, our present social arrangements, such as marriage and family, will be continued. God ensures eternal bliss of an absolute kind. That should be enough.

5. One of the great differences from our present life is that in eternity we can relate to God in an immediate way. The "veil" between God and us has been lifted. At last it will become reality what we so often sing: "Face to face shall I behold Him!" At last Christ is the center of all things.

God must have had a purpose in not providing us with a more detailed description of the destiny of humankind—of this planet and of the universe. Apparently, He does not want us to spend all our time and energy in speculation about what will be, in the same way that millions of people across the world now spend a major portion of their time in their obsessions with a "virtual" existence in a "second life" in the world of the Internet. God wants us to experience a basic assurance that in the end all will be well. Heaven will come. There is an ultimate destination that is reality. While we are still here in the present, this gives significance to our day-to-day activities.[10] In that limited sense heaven can already be ours while we continue to faithfully serve Him here.

---

[1] A very accessible overview is given by Colleen McDannell and Bernhard Lang in *Heaven—A History* (New Haven, Conn.: Yale University Press, 1990).

[2] Arthur L. White, *Ellen G. White: The Early Years* (Hagerstown, Md.: Review and Herald Pub. Assn., 1985), pp. 56ff.

[3] Ellen G. White, *Maranatha*, p. 309.

[4] See Walton J. Brown, *Home at Last* (Hagerstown, Md.: Review and Herald Pub. Assn., 1983). p. 36, 37.

[5] *Ibid.*, p. 55.

[6] Ellen G. White, *The Great Controversy*, pp. 674, 675.

[7] H. Richard Niebuhr, *The Kingdom of God in America*, p. 135.

[8] Richard Harries, *God Outside the Box: Why Spiritual People Object to Christianity* (London: SPCK, 2002), pp. 28-32.

[9] For the following paragraph I am much indebted to H. Berkhof, *Christelijk Geloof* (Nijkerk: G. F. Callenbach BV, 1973), pp. 556-564.

[10] Richard Rice, *Reign of God* (Berrien Springs, Mich.: Andrews University Press, 1997), p. 346.

DISCIPLESHIP 10

"How can you hope to enter into communion with Him when at some point in your life you are running away from Him?"

—DIETRICH BONHOEFFER, *The Cost of Discipleship,* p. 73

What is a disciple? It does not take much Bible study to see that while Scripture employs the word for the 12 men who formed a close circle around Jesus, it also has a much more general and wider meaning. In Acts 11:26 we read that Jesus' followers in the Syrian city of Antioch were the first to be called Christians. Here the New Living Translation correctly uses the word "believers," whereas many other versions refer to "disciples." Clearly in this context "disciple" does not apply just to a small elite of leaders, but to all members of the church. The Greek word usually translated as "disciple" occurs some 250 times in the gospels and in the book of Acts. In many cases it does, indeed, refer to "the twelve" whom Jesus called at the beginning of His earthly ministry to be with Him and be trained by Him. But Scripture refers to many others also as disciples. The New Testament employs the word for the followers of John the Baptist (John 3:24ff.) and of the Pharisees (Mark 2:18), and we hear of people described as "disciples" of Moses (John 9:28). Other followers besides "the twelve" were disciples of Jesus. Take, for instance, Joseph of Arimathea, whom John called "a secret disciple" of Jesus (John 19:38). But also remember the 72 disciples sent out on a short-term mission assignment (Luke 10:1). Many

Bible versions label Tabitha, the woman from Joppa who excelled in humanitarian activities, as a disciple (Acts 9:36). This is also true of the followers of Paul, who helped him escape from Damascus (Acts 9:25).

The fact that Scripture does not restrict discipleship to a small group among the believers is also abundantly clear from the gospel commission that Jesus gave to His church after His resurrection: "Go and make disciples" (Matt. 28:19). The implication is that discipleship was to be the privilege of every believer in Christ.

What is a disciple?

Being a disciple means following a master. Masters with followers were a widespread phenomenon in the ancient world, and even today we hear of gurus and other masters who recruit disciples as their followers. In Judaism many rabbis acquired a following of disciples during the period between the Old and the New Testament and in Jesus' day, much as the Greek philosophers did.

The relationship between master and disciple is one of inequality. "A student is not greater than the teacher" (Luke 6:40), even though students may aspire to become like their teachers. In a purely human situation, students may actually succeed or eventually surpass their teachers. As far as Christ and His disciples are concerned, the fundamental inequality in the relationship will always continue to exist. He is and remains the Lord, whose authority we must recognize and who continues to demand our obedience and loyalty. The oft-used metaphor of the master and his "slaves" underscores this in a powerful way.

The fundamental element of discipleship is learning. The Greek word *mathetes,* traditionally translated as "disciple," stands for "student" or "learner" and derives from a verb that means "to learn." The 12 disciples, who were to have an essential role in the new Jesus movement, went through a three-year learning process. Teaching and learning are part and parcel of everything involving discipleship. New disciples are to be "taught" before they are baptized (Matt. 28:18). The Gospels portray Jesus not only as a preacher or miracle worker, but also as a teacher. "Anyone," Jesus said, "who listens to my teachings . . . is wise" (Matt. 7:24). His many parables offer sublime examples of the depth of His teaching. While in Capernaum He habitually taught in the local synagogue. It impressed the people, for "he spoke with authority' (Luke 4:32). When the spiritual leaders of the day queried the guards of the Temple why they had done nothing to curtail Jesus' influence, they replied that they had simply been too impressed, for, they said, "We have never heard anyone talk like this!" (John 7:46).

Through the teachings delivered to us in the gospels Christ continues to be our teacher. The success of the teaching process does not, however, rest only on the availability of a first-rate instructor. It depends just as much on the willingness of the learners to concentrate on what they hear and their willingness to absorb and apply those teachings. In other words, those who want to be disciples today must be teachable. They must be open to Jesus' teachings, and they must resolve to apply them in their daily life, as they fulfill their part in Christ's mission.

Discipleship also contains the element of *imitation*. The learning that takes place should result in internalizing the values of the kingdom that Christ teaches. "The student who works hard will become *like* the teacher" (Luke 6:40). This is, of course, not true in its absolute sense in our Christian discipleship career. We will never become as perfect and as wise as our Teacher. Yet, He is the supreme role model whom we will be eager to emulate. Discipleship will change us and will have visible results. "My true disciples produce much fruit," Jesus stated, when calling Himself "the true vine" and comparing His followers to the "branches" that are supposed to bear abundant fruit (John 15:8). Discipleship becomes tangible in our stewardship approach toward all aspects of life. (We will focus on that aspect in the next chapter.) Therefore, Jesus challenges His disciples to be the light of the world, offering an example that all can see. At the same time they are the salt of the earth, which gives flavor to all and everything they come into contact with.

Caring for other members of the faith community is another aspect of discipleship. Christ told the disciples to love one another, as He had loved them. "Your love for one another," He explained, "will prove to the world that you are my disciples" (John 13:35). *Obedience* is another key word when we try to analyze what discipleship entails. When we "make" disciples, we must teach them to obey all Christ's commandments (Matt. 28:19, 20). That is the bottom line of the message of grace: a response of willing obedience.

Some of the disciples around Christ became apostles and fulfilled leadership roles in the early church. But it was not limited to the 12 that Jesus called when He began His ministry. In fact, one of these men became a traitor rather than an apostle. Paul, on the other hand, who was not among the original 12, claimed to have the ranking of an apostle in spite of the fact that some disputed it. His converts, he maintained, were "a living proof that [he was] the Lord's apostle" (1 Cor. 9:2). And many others, Paul wrote, were to receive the spiritual gift of apostleship (1 Cor. 12:28). But though not all disciples would become apostles, all would be involved in fulfilling the mission of Christ.

Becoming a disciple

Discipleship involves discipline. In the Christian life discipline has two basic levels. We may differentiate between "spiritual" discipline and "common-sense" discipline. Almost from the beginning of the Christian Era some people have pursued an ascetic lifestyle as a way to get close to God. The fifth- and sixth-century pillar saints who withdrew into the Syrian deserts and who spent days and nights, often during many years, on top of a pillar are extreme examples. They dedicated their life to rigorous fasting and constant prayer. Their goal was to receive assurance of the salvation of their souls through the mortification of their body. In the Middle Ages some monks and nuns wanted to be enclosed in small cloister cells, totally isolated from the world around them. This, they believed, would help them reach the ultimate unity with the divine that they longed for. Ignatius of Loyola (1491-1556), the founder of the Jesuit order, wrote the famous *Spiritual Exercises*, a collection of meditations, prayers, and mental exercises. Such daily instructions, designed to be carried out over a period of about a month, included various contemplations on the nature of the world, of human psychology as Ignatius understood it, and of humanity's relationship to God. Many Catholics still use them as a method of attaining a closer walk with God. Today Christians of all persuasions attend retreats, go on pilgrimages, or spend time in total isolation as a means of strengthening their spiritual life and reinforcing their commitment to discipleship.

Protestants tend to be suspicious of most of such spiritual "works," and often with good reason. As Seventh-day Adventists we belong to a segment of Christianity in which activism has always had more admirers than systematic meditation and extended spiritual seclusion. Yet, we do recognize—or at least we should—that the life of a disciple needs constant spiritual nourishment. Increasingly the church realizes that, while evangelistic outreach (preaching) may be strong, the teaching and nurturing of new believers sadly often gets neglected. As a result, many newly baptized people do not move on to the stage of real discipleship. Also, many of us who claim to be disciples fail to nourish our discipleship sufficiently. We do not need thick manuals with set prayers and all kinds of prescribed activities in order to lift our spirit heavenward. That is not how the Spirit, who is like a wind that "blows" in ways beyond our control, operates (John 3:8). However, it does not mean that most of us do not need a lot more discipline in our spiritual lives. Allotting time for regular Bible *reading* (not just Bible *study*, but also the systematic *reading* of the Word), making sure that prayer is a fundamental part of our daily routine, and dialogue with other believers (reinforced by reading carefully selected books that will enrich our understanding) are all parts of a nonnegotiable foundation for solid discipleship.

At the same time, there are "common sense" elements in our intentional fostering of discipleship. Perhaps we may sum them up as subordinating the lesser to the greater. Life must be a process of constant and conscious choice, and not a mere drifting along in whatever way the stream happens to flow. For example, we cannot see everything, listen to everything, read everything, go everywhere, and investigate everything. We do not have the time, and we usually do not have the energy or the resources for that. It is essential that we say no to some things and eagerly embrace other things. Life demands choices and the constant setting of priorities. It may help us if we learn to master certain skills, ask others for advice more frequently, or take certain precautions, in our intentional pursuit of a life of disciplined discipleship.

The cost of discipleship

Being a disciple is a privilege and a blessing. Discipleship brings inner peace and produces inestimable joy. It binds us together in a meaningful fellowship with others who share the same ideals and loyalties. But we were never told it would all be easy. In fact, Christ never made any effort to hide the fact that discipleship could be costly, because it may require making difficult choices, establishing painful priorities, and offering costly sacrifices. Few statements about the cost of discipleship are more straightforward than the words of Christ that I want to quote at some length:

"Don't imagine that I came to bring peace to the earth! No, I came to bring a sword. I have come to set a man against his father, a daughter against her mother, and a daughter-in-law against her mother-in-law. Your enemies will be right in your own household!

"If you love your father or mother more than you love me, you are not worthy of being mine; or if you love your son or daughter more than me, you are not worthy of being mine. If you refuse to take up your cross and follow me, you are not worthy of being mine. If you cling to your life, you will lose it; but if you give it up for me, you will find it" (Matt. 10:34-39).

Being a disciple means always giving the Master first and total allegiance. He comes before and above everything and everyone else, including those dearest to us. Following Christ may mean ridicule and rejection—or worse—but so be it. It is all worth it!

The disciples who became apostles especially experienced the cost of discipleship. The Bible records the martyr's death of only one apostle—James, the brother of John, by the sword of the servants of King Herod (Acts 12:1). But ancient traditions give us reason to believe that at least seven other apostles suffered a martyr's death. Simon Peter and Paul are said to have died in Rome during the

Neronian persecution (A.D. 67 or 68). Church Father Origen (c. 185-c. 254) says that Peter felt himself to be unworthy to be put to death in the same manner as his Master, and was therefore, at his own request, crucified with his head downward. Andrew, Philip, Matthew, Thaddaeus, Simon the Zealot, and Thomas also reportedly paid for their loyalty to Christ with their lives. Traditions that go back to the fourth century say that Thomas preached in Parthia or Persia, and was finally buried at Edessa in Syria. Later traditions carry him even farther east. His martyrdom, whether in Persia or India, is said to have been by a lance, and is still commemorated each year by the Latin Church on December 21, by the Greek Church on October 6, and by Indian believers on July 1.

Before Paul arrived in Rome to face imprisonment and death he experienced more hardships and persecution than one would believe a single person can survive without giving up. The catalog of his sufferings sounds like an absolute record of human endurance: "I have worked harder, been put in jail more often, been whipped times without number, and faced death again and again. Five different times the Jews gave me thirty-nine lashes. Three times I was beaten with rods. Once I was stoned. Three times I was shipwrecked." And so the list of horror goes on (see 2 Cor. 11:23-26). The apostles were just at the beginning of the interminable line of millions who, through the centuries, have paid the highest possible price for the privilege of discipleship. And do not for a moment think this is all a thing of the past—that in the twenty-first century we live in an enlightened age in which almost all nations officially recognize religious freedom. The truth is that today some 60 different countries harass, abuse, arrest, torture, and sometimes execute Christians because of their faith. Some 200 million Christians around the world live in daily fear of the secret police or other agents of repression and discrimination.* And no one knows what the future holds. If the end-time scenario that Adventists believe in comes anywhere near the truth, a time of great horror (Matt. 24:21) will test the patience of God's people to the very limit of their power to endure (Rev. 14:12).

Even today in the Western world discipleship may be costly.

Obedience to God may run contrary to the loyalty that our boss or our colleagues expect from us. Sticking up for principle may result in a lost promotion and missed career opportunities. And discipleship can take its toll on our relationships when we have to make sure that other people, even our loved ones, do not get in the way of our commitment to our Lord. But whatever the price is, it is not beyond what we can endure as long as we trust in God. We must remember that if it gets rough, we are not the only ones who must pay the cost of discipleship: "The temptations that come into your life are no different from what others experience" (1 Cor. 10:13). That in itself would be little comfort. But there is more: "God is faithful. He will keep the temptation from becoming so strong that you can't stand up against it. When you are tempted, he will show you a way out so that you will not give in to it" (verse 13). And finally, we must never forget that, whatever price we are asked to pay, that which God paid to save us was infinitely greater!

---

* See, e.g., Paul Marshall, *Their Blood Cries Out* (Nashville: W Publishing Group, 1997).

STEWARDSHIP   11

"There is more religion in a good loaf of bread than many think."
—ELLEN G. WHITE, *Counsels on Diet and Foods*, p. 316

One of the deplorable aspects of the postmodern philosophy is, I think, the predilection for fragmentation. Whenever Jacques Derrida (1930-2004), one of the famous postmodern philosophers, would be asked "How are you?" he would respond with the counterquestion: "At what floor?" He liked to compare his life with a house with several floors, each with a number of rooms, and the life he lived in one room would be quite different from how he lived in another.

This trend toward fragmentation, unfortunately, is also leaving its traces in many Christian lives. The values that direct the life of Christians when at home may differ greatly from how they live when in church. And then again, they may show another kind of conduct when working out at the gym or operating in the workplace. Naturally, the roles we "play" will always affect how we act and speak. Yet Christianity ought to determine who and what we are in a 24/7 way. That is what discipleship is all about, as we saw in the previous chapter. But it also lies at the basis of the concept of *stewardship*. Both Christians and non-Christians use the word, but it has a far more profound meaning for those who want to model their life after that of Christ. Being a steward is not something that happens just on one floor or in one room of our existence—it affects every area of our life.

Most essays or sermons about stewardship take their point of departure in the story Jesus told about the three servants in Matthew 25 and a similar account in Luke 19. The dramatis personae differ, but the intent of the two accounts is the same. A "master" who went on a trip abroad left a varying amount of money (or "talents") to each of his servants. Upon his return he was eager to find out what profit the servants had made. Those who had produced a healthy gain on what they had been entrusted received praise, while the one servant who had not made any profit, because he had only jealously guarded what he had been given without putting it to any use, faced severe criticism. The lesson is clear: We have the responsibility to use our resources in the best possible way. It is not just a matter of common sense—it is a religious duty. What we have is not simply ours, but has been entrusted to us for optimal use. We must therefore look after it and do our utmost to make a "profit."

Whenever the topic of stewardship gets discussed, it will soon touch on monetary issues. That is only natural, for money plays a crucial role in human life—as well as in the life of a Christian. But it would be a serious misunderstanding to limit the realm of stewardship to material matters. It has to do with many other areas of life: our skills and capabilities, the use of our intellect and our potential influence in society, our time management, our health, and most definitely responsibility for our planet—the climate and nature and natural resources.

Stewards of the world

It is good to see that many Adventist Christians are deeply interested in the world in which they live and participate in politics as well as in efforts to safeguard nature, to keep our world clean, to do what they can to counter climate change, and to be careful with the finite resources of our planet. Yet it would seem that early Adventism was in many ways ahead of current Adventism in its societal concerns. It is truly surprising to see how a small emerging religious community that still had to invest so much of its energy in establishing its doctrinal identity and to get organizationally off the ground could, at the same time, be so involved in initiatives to oppose slavery, in defending the noncombatancy principle in the midst of a Civil War, and, even more so, in assuming a leading role in temperance campaigns, in being at the front line in health reform, and in courageously facing religious liberty challenges. Early Adventists, in spite of their emphasis on a soon return of Christ, had not withdrawn from the world, but were keen to profile themselves strongly as stewards of the world. Considering this rich heritage of involvement in society, one wonders what happened and what caused so much of this active stewardship involvement with the world around us to disappear gradually.

Christians who place great value on the creation story should pay special attention to the stewardship implications of the first few chapters in Genesis, for that is where the foundation for the stewardship concept is laid. It all starts in the Garden of Eden. God blessed the first couple He had created, and then gave them their task: "Multiply and fill the earth, and subdue it. Be masters over the fish and birds and all the animals" (Gen. 1:28). We might paraphrase "subdue it" as "harness its potential." Humanity received the assignment to look after God's creation. "The Lord God placed the man in the Garden of Eden to tend and care for it" (Gen. 2:15). Significantly, Adam had to give names to all God's creatures. It indicates that he was to have control over them. Note that our responsibility toward the earth is that of the tending of a garden—it is not a license to exploit or plunder the creation of God. Unfortunately, humanity has not handled that job very well. Rather then "tending" the earth and caring for it, human beings have exploited and destroyed a large portion of what they were supposed to protect. Examples abound. The tropical rain forest has been decimated, with huge profits disappearing into the deep pockets of Western businessmen and corrupt politicians of developing countries. The reserves of fossil fuels are rapidly depleting, recklessly releasing huge amounts of carbon dioxide into the atmosphere and most probably providing the main cause for dramatic climate changes. Human beings are genetically "improving" God's creation and have been adding so many substances to the soil, to animal feed, and to his own food that the average person is now at a loss to determine what is safe to eat and what is dangerous to consume.

It may be impossible to redress many of the processes threatening the environment. After all, it is an undeniable fact that the ultimate solution for the problems of our planet must come from above. Yet it is never too late for Christians to assume their responsibilities, individually and collectively, in championing a stewardship lifestyle. And even if the results can only be incremental, and even if all combined stewardship efforts will not undo the damage already done, it is the Christian's duty to give a signal that God is the owner and that we are to recognize His ownership visibly and concretely. A church community that speaks so much of stewardship may need to reevaluate what it presently actually does, and what it should and could do. Rather than being the head among today's organizations that call for a more responsible attitude toward the earth and its resources, the shameful reality seems that we are closer to the tail. Too often we have limited our view of stewardship to a few health rules and a few monetary issues. For Bible Christians that is simply not good enough.

Is our body our own?

The idea of being stewards of our body may appeal more to many Christians today than it did in the past. Traditionally many Christians insisted that faith has to do with your soul and not in any direct way with your body. As a result, it was amazing to see how many Christians abused their body. Smoking, the use of alcohol, and dietary carelessness were just as much part of many a Christian home as they were elsewhere. It would seem that in this respect some progress has been made, as people in general have learned more about healthful living and many Christians have also begun to see themselves in a more wholistic way, with body and spirit more closely interacting than previously recognized.

About one thing Christians should have no doubt. Their body is not their own property to use or abuse as they see fit. The apostle Paul asked the Corinthians a question that remains relevant for us: "Don't you know that your body is the temple of the Holy Spirit?"

(1 Cor. 6:19). The implication is unequivocal: "So you must honor God with your body" (verse 20).

Although the focus of the Bible is, indeed, primarily on our spiritual life and nurture, Scripture does not consider the body unimportant. The Old Testament contains many laws and instructions on hygiene and food preparation. It differentiates between foods fit for human consumption and those not (Lev. 11). Remarks about our physical well-being abound in such books as Proverbs and Ecclesiastes. Jesus showed a consistent interest in humanity's physical welfare. He healed many people who suffered from a great variety of illnesses, and even raised several from death. And He did not feel that it was beneath the dignity of a famous rabbi also, when necessary, to provide adequate catering for the masses that came to Him to listen.

Adventist theology has, as we noted, almost from the very beginning stressed the fundamental unity of the human being, pointing to the Creation account that declares that the first man became a "living person" after the breath of life had entered the material "stuff" that God had prepared (Gen. 2:7). From very early on in their existence Adventists have rejected the duality of body and soul, as commonly accepted by most other Christians. And from early on they were extremely interested in health reform. They soon rejected all use of alcoholic beverages and tobacco. The taboo on other drugs followed suit. Also, from an early date, the vegetarian lifestyle received strong support in preference even to a diet that would not touch the food that the Bible referred to as "clean."

Health surveys in many countries have provided irrefutable evidence, time and again, that the Adventist lifestyle offers many health benefits, even though they could have an even greater impact if more Adventists would be more careful in their lifestyle choices. The suggestion often heard that a majority of Adventists have opted for a vegetarian lifestyle is one of those myths about Adventism that somehow live on. Research indicates that the percentage of vegetarians among Adventists currently stands at approximately 28 percent. It is doubtful whether it has ever been much higher, except in certain specific geographical areas!*

All in all, one might say that Adventists have done reasonably well in giving substance to the stewardship of their body. Yet many of us can and should do better. More Adventists suffer from obesity than one would expect of a community that strives for a healthy lifestyle. It is doubtful that Adventists have fewer workaholics and fewer victims of burnout than among the general population. Many of us know that we do not get enough exercise, eat lots of fast foods, and take in far too much sugar. While many of us do "obey" the traditional health rules that we have grown up with, if we are really honest many of us should also admit that we are not as health-conscious as we could be. As a denomination, we are still very much into the business of health. We maintain high standards in most of our institutions. But have we, possibly, lost too much of our early willingness to be on the front lines of the pursuit for a healthier life? Should we, possibly, rekindle at least to some extent our former enthusiasm for natural remedies, and become a bit more reluctant toward the use of synthetic medicines with their numerous side effects? Should we, possibly, be a little more outspoken about the way that much of our food gets processed? Should we, possibly, be a bit more alarmed about some of the things that happen to our food, both from animal as well as nonanimal sources? And should we, possibly, depend a bit more on the vitamins and other vital elements in our food rather than rely so much on the supplements that have become so omnipresent on our tables? Should we, possibly, rethink what it would really mean for each of us individually to be a faithful steward of our bodys?

Time management

Religion affects how we spend our time. Time is a serious and valuable commodity. In our present life it has a definite limit. "Seventy years are given to us!" the psalmist tells us. "Some may even reach eighty. . . . Soon they disappear and we are gone" (Ps. 90:10). But this does not mean that every moment must be useful in the material sense in which we normally employ the word. Christ often had a full program. Yet in the midst of His travels and teachings He was very much a people person. He had time to talk, time for a good meal, time for a party, and time for recreation. If we want to imitate Him, that should also set the pattern for us. On the one hand, it is important to avoid those things that waste our time and energy and do not enrich our own or anyone else's life. On the other hand, we must remember that life is more than work and that we should take time for things we can truly enjoy.

God created time in cycles of six plus one, and it still remains humanity's basic life rhythm. Six days for work and all kinds of other common things, and one day set aside by God as "holy" time. It has proved to be a schedule that suits our human needs wonderfully.

The many books written on time management all emphasize not only the need for planning—short-term, midterm and long-term— but also to establish priorities and to maintain balance. Ecclesiastes 3 is a unique summary of the kind of balance that helps a Christian live a full life. It offers time not only for work but also for recreation and rest. There is a time for church work, but also time for friends and family. And while there is time for others, we must also have time for ourselves.

Talents and/or spiritual gifts?

Adolf Hitler was probably one of the greatest monsters of the twentieth century, if not of all time. Yet many obeyed and even worshipped him. Why? How was it possible he commanded such a massive following? Without doubt he had some great talents—in particular, that of oratory. He could move the masses. Martin Luther King, who played such a pivotal role in the civil rights movement in the United States, had some of the same gifts. For generations people will remember his famous speech: "I have a dream that one day . . ." Both Hitler and King were extremely talented and could move hundreds of thousands by their gift of oratory. What was the difference? Hitler was power-hungry, filled with hatred, and served himself. King put his talents into the service of a holy cause and served others. That made all the difference.

The Bible not only refers to "talents," but also speaks of "spiritual gifts." All believers, Scripture tells us, are equipped with some gift. Some of these are very special, even dramatic: the gift of healing, of speaking in tongues, of preaching. Other spiritual gifts appear more mundane: teaching, counseling, sound administration, providing help and comfort, etc. A number of passages list the various ones: Romans 12, Ephesians 4, 1 Corinthians 12-15, and elsewhere. Commentators differ as to whether the list totals 22 (or fewer) gifts. We can divide them into (1) teaching/leadership gifts, (2) service gifts, and (3) "sign" gifts (given to authenticate the work of apostles and prophets, particularly when God wanted the early church to be established and grow).

The Bible does not tell us what the exact difference is between talents and gifts. It appears that they overlap to a considerable extent. Perhaps "talent" refers in particular to the genetic aspect, and to the process of learning and developing certain skills, whereas "gift" emphasizes the divine grace of bestowing certain possibilities on us, even when we lack a natural giftedness in such areas. Whatever be the case, the skills we have developed and the gifts that God has entrusted us with should be fused in our Christian witness in word and deed.

The marvelous thing is not only that we all have talents and gifts, but also that those talents and gifts differ widely. We see this in ordinary life. Some are artistic, while others have a talent for business. Some are good cooks, while playing football is not the area where they can excel. Some can lead in worship through song, while others had better stay away from attempting it. But they may be great storytellers! None of us can do everything well. We always need others and must learn to function as team members. It applies not only to our professional life but church life as well.

While it is essential to know our limitations, it is just as crucial to be aware of our God-given potential and to be a good steward over this aspect of our lives. None of the Bible passages about the "talents" ever suggest that every skill and capability we have should be overtly religious. Not every song we can sing must be a religious hymn, not every poem we may write needs to be about God, and not every aspect of our organizational skills has to be directed at the church. But we can use all our talents and gifts, whether in the areas of sport, gardening, cooking, or computers and business, to the glory of God. "*Whatever* you do, you must do all for the glory of God" (1 Cor. 10:31). The question you must simply continue to ask is: Is what I do pleasing to God? Does it enrich my life? Does it give true joy and satisfaction to me and others? Does it make the world just a tiny little bit better or more beautiful? Does it make others around me happy? Is what I do fitting for someone who belongs in the camp of God? Does it affirm my commitment to Him, or steer me away from Him?

Money

Finally, let's think about material things, money in particular. Consider just a few basic principles. First of all—and this is true of all we have—God is the owner and what we have we only have in loan. The very fact of His creatorship implies this. When the well-known evangelical songwriter John W. Peterson (1921-2006) contemplated Psalm 50:10, the famous text about God's ownership, he wrote about how the Lord possesses the cattle on a thousand hills, the landscape itself and the wealth in it, and the sky above. We find this basic thought also clearly expressed in Jesus' story about the *owner* of a given vineyard in trust to tenant farmers, and about the servants and the owner's son who came to check on the work of the tenants. The underlying relationships are abundantly clear: there is an undisputed owner, and there are tenants (Matt. 21:33-46).

The second biblical principle about the stewardship of our material possessions appears in a saying of Christ recorded in Acts 20:35: "It is more blessed to give than to receive." Such a concept goes against the grain of human nature, but it is a truth that experience has proved to be true time and again. However, only real selflessness qualifies as this kind of giving. It does not seek to establish a reputation for generosity, nor is it motivated mainly by fiscal advantages. The "blessed" kind of giving is not expressed in dollar signs, but in the amount of love that propels it. That is why there was something fatally wrong with the generous gift of Ananias and Sapphira (Acts 5:1-10) and why, on the other hand, Jesus greatly appreciated the two pennies of the poor widow (Mark 12:41-44) and the effusion of expensive perfume (John 12:1-7).

Giving is not an awkward, painful aspect of stewardship, but it epitomizes its joys. God looks for a "willing gift," not for one given under subtle or not-so-subtle pressure (2 Cor. 9:7). He wants us to look after those in need and not to be hard-hearted or tightfisted (Deut.

15:7). Also He wants us to be generous when we consider our gifts to Him. This brings us to the third fundamental principle: God has a first right to anything that we may decide to do with our "possessions." We should "return" a significant part of what He has lent us as an unmistakable acknowledgment that all that we have received is His. The Old Testament established a minimum norm for our giving to God of 10 percent. The New Testament refers only a few times in passing to the giving of tithes (as, for instance, in Matthew 23:23). Tithing, apparently, is so natural that it needs no further discussion.

Considering all we know now, as New Testament Christians, about the divine love that has no limit, it seems hardly appropriate to even consider giving less to God than what the Old Testament taught believers to do. Therefore, there is every reason to continue quoting the famous passage in the prophetic writings of Malachi (3:8-13). The prophet warns God's people not to "cheat" by withholding their tithes. He challenges them—and us—to "bring all the tithes into the storehouse" (verse 10). The promise of the Almighty is awaiting all who will do so: "I will open the windows of heaven for you. I will pour out a blessing so great you won't have enough room to take it in! Try it! Let me prove it to you!" (verse 10).

Christian stewardship has wide dimensions. It is a matter of choice. We either serve Him and recognize Him for what He is, or we turn our backs on Him and focus on ourselves. "No one can serve two masters" (Matt. 6:24). Either He is our Lord or He is not. And we can be true disciples and recognize His lordship only if we prove to be good stewards. The two concepts are totally intertwined.

Of course, none of the things we have mentioned will help us earn our eternal reward. We are saved through faith in Jesus Christ, not by recycling our glass or paper; by purchasing a "clean" car; by pursuing the healthiest possible diet; faithfully taking piano lessons to develop our musical talents; or by never forgetting to give our tithe. But commitment to Jesus Christ will become visible in the way it operates in our daily lives (James 2:18). That is what stewardship is all about.

★ Keith Lockhart, "The Myth of Vegetarianism," *Spectrum* 34, no. 1 (winter 2006): 22-28.

COMMUNITY 12

"The church is God's family; adopted by Him as children, its members live on the basis of the new covenant. The church is the body of Christ, a community of faith of which Christ Himself is the Head. The church is the bride for whom Christ died that He might sanctify and cleanse her. At His return in triumph, He will present her to Himself a glorious church, the faithful of all ages, the purchase of His blood, not having spot or wrinkle, but holy and without blemish."

—*Fundamental Beliefs of Seventh-day Adventists,* no. 12

Many people in today's world, especially in the West, are increasingly interested in spirituality, but are highly suspicious of the institutional church. Not so sure whether we actually need organized religion with all the baggage it allegedly brings along, they ask: Do we still need the church? For many, the fact that Christianity has proliferated into thousands of fragments, each promoting its own variety of truth and defending particular rites and traditions, is an enormous stumbling stone. It seems a far cry from the unity Christ told His followers to pray for. If we need the church, where is the church? In all the separate Christian traditions, or only in one segment that has "the truth"?

Also, increasingly, people who request baptism do not want to join a particular church community. Is this biblically defensible? Should a denomination demand that its new members subscribe to a long list of doctrines, or be willing to baptize anyone who simply expresses a desire to follow Christ, whether he or she wants to belong to its visible community or not?

Other questions abound. What kind of church organization has the best papers? Should local congregations have total autonomy? Or is a national, or even global, structure more in harmony with biblical principles? How do the roles of the clergy and the laity relate? And what about the ordination of women to church offices and pastoral ministry? How can, or should, church discipline function in today's world? How do para-church entities fit into a biblical concept of church? How should we define the concept of a remnant? And so the list continues.

Community—a biblical concept

God has always wanted to work through a community of people. Even before He made His covenant with Abraham and promised him that he would be the progenitor of a special nation that would be a blessing for the entire world (Gen. 12:1-3), the Lord singled out particular families in the lineage of Adam, Seth, Noah, and Shem as the guardians of His truth.

In the Old Testament God spoke of the people of Israel as His "holy people" (Deut. 28:9), and as a "holy nation." The New Testament described His followers as a "congregation" or "assembly" that has been called out (Acts 7:38). The Septuagint (the ancient Greek translation of the Old Testament in use at the time of Christ) often employs the word *ekklesia* to refer to God's people of old. There it translates the Hebrew word *qahal*, which has a root meaning of "being called." The Greek word *ekklesia* is a composite of two words: *ek* ("out") and the verb *kalein* ("to call"). God summoned His Old Testament people for a specific mission: to proclaim their God to the other nations around them (Isa. 56:7).

The calling of the disciples (Mark 3:13-19) marked the first stage of the creation of the New Testament community of believers. Twelve key followers of Jesus constituted an elite group who received a special role. The 12 had the privilege of receiving extensive training through their association with Jesus (Mark 6:7-12; Matt. 9:35-10:18). Note, however, that the Gospels refer to more persons as "disciples" of Christ, including the 72 disciples that Jesus sent out on a special mission (Luke 10:1-24) and several women (see, for instance, Luke 8:1-3).

During the last supper (Matt. 26:26-29 and parallel passages) Christ instituted the "new covenant" with His disciples as the new people of God. This Bible passage is important not just because of its bearing on the institution and meaning of the Lord's Supper, but also for the wider concept of the community that would practice this solemn rite henceforth until Christ's second coming.

The church would not just be an association of people who would enjoy social activities or meet regularly for spiritual edification. God established the church because He had a mission for it to accomplish. The mission is, in fact, *the* reason the church exists. The Great Commission (Matt. 28:19, 20 and parallel passages in the other gospels) is not without good reason the climax of the gospel story.

Immediately after the departure of the Lord we discover a community of believers in Jerusalem, with the disciples as its key figures. The fragmentary information in Acts 2:42-47 suggests some form of communal life, but also continuous growth. Even members of the Jewish clergy joined the Christ believers (Acts 6:7). The outpouring of the Spirit during the feast of Pentecost provided the supernatural infusion of power that catapulted the Christian community onto the first-century religious scene. Visitors from many different regions heard the good news of Christ in their own languages and took their new insights with them when they returned home. Opposition led to a further dispersion of believers in Judea and Samaria (Acts 8:1). Acts 8 reports the activities of Philip in Samaria and his contacts with a dignitary who was on his way back to Nubia. Acts 9 describes the progress of the church in Damascus. And so the story continues. From the beginning the church was ethnically and culturally diverse, and as it expanded, so did its organizational structure.

What is the church?

The New Testament speaks about the church as well as about the kingdom of God. Are these two identical? Almost, but not quite. The church is the human community that lives under God's rule. One might say: the kingdom creates the church and the church, in turn, witnesses to the kingdom, and lives on the basis of the ethics of the kingdom, as expressed in the teachings of Christ on the mount of blessing.

One traditional Christian view (still widely held) is that the church has *replaced* Israel in God's plan. Theologians usually label the concept as the *substitution theory*. In this context many often refer to the church as the "spiritual Israel." Although that term does not appear in the New Testament, it is believed, also by a majority of Adventist theologians, that the New Testament evidence amply supports the idea. Some Adventist scholars argue, however, that the supporters of the substitution theory overstate their case and that we find sufficient biblical basis to defend a continuing role for the Jews in the salvific (salvation-historical) purposes of God. It would seem that, at the very least, we must recognize continuity as well as discontinuity between Israel and the church.

An invisible church?

Often people make a distinction between the *invisible* and the *visible* church. The invisible church supposedly consists of those believers who have already passed to their rest, of those who will yet be born and will choose to believe, and of all those believers who now live anywhere on the earth and may or may not be members of Christian communities. While unknown to us, they are known to Him who "sees every heart" (1 Chron. 28:9) and "knows . . . who are his" (2 Tim. 2:19). In some traditions, such as the Roman Catholic Church and the Orthodox churches, the distinction between the invisible and the visible church (their own church) is rather blurred, and we detect at times a tendency to let the two coincide. Other Christian groups, the Adventist Church among them, insist that there exists not only an invisible church but also a visible community, and that it is important for individual believers to join the visible community if at all possible. This, of course, raises the question as to whether Christians who live in a particular region must all join one particular church entity if they want to be part of the people of God and are to be saved.

Very few denominations restrict the visible church on earth to their own organization. Seventh-day Adventists have never held this position either. They see the church as wider than their own denomination. Yet not everything that calls itself "church" qualifies as such. The New Testament is clear about the reality of apostasy. There are situations in which false doctrine gets taught, and "false prophets" do lead people astray. When Christ is no longer worshipped as Lord, and apostasy has reached beyond a certain point (1 John 4:1-6), there is no doubt that the situation has gone beyond the confines of Christ's church. Passages such as 1 Timothy 4:1-5 and 2 Timothy 3:1-9 are among the most outspoken statements regarding the reality of apostasy, in particular in "the last days." So not every visible institution that calls itself "church" can, in fact, claim to be part of God's visible church. Christians need the "gift of discernment" to know when error has so obscured the truth that we may safely conclude that one can no longer regard a particular tradition, group, or organization as part of the Christian church (1 Cor. 12:10). In those cases one may speak of "apostate Christianity," and one would be justified in using such labels as "sect" or "cult." However, even then one must take care not to pronounce judgment on individual believers. And we must never forget that Christ warned us not to try to sit in judgment and make a precise division between what is true and what is false, for our human judgment will never be fully trustworthy (Matt. 13:24-30, 36-43). Our focus should be on our own efforts to follow and proclaim truth. This is what official Adventism has always believed.

But Adventists also believe that a special segment of the visible church has a unique place and role. Here we meet the concept of the *remnant*, a term already found in the Old Testament—in particular in the prophetic writings—but given a specific application in the end-time setting. At the end of time there is a "rest" (Rev. 12:17) of those who remain loyal to their Creator and keep God's commandments. Adventists believe that in the final climax of history the visible church will coincide with that faithful "rest." The Adventist end-time scenario predicts a growing opposition between the "true" church and the "apostate" church. Large sections of Christianity will eventually be part of "Babylon," while a relatively small part of Christianity will stand firm in its obedience to Bible truth. Here is where Seventh-day Adventists see their special role and mission. This has been both a blessing and a temptation. Adventist eschatology has helped the church to understand its responsibility and global mission. But it has also tended to encourage people to look at the church primarily as a place for the few who are saved and as a community of (almost) perfect saints who "have" the truth, rather than as a school for sinners. As a result it has often fostered a tendency toward perfectionism and legalism.

Tradition and truth

We have the truth of the Bible, while other churches are ensnared in their human traditions! Few would be prepared to express their conviction quite as bluntly as this, yet it is what many Adventists in fact think. And, indeed, there is no doubt that inherited traditions rather than any independent personal study of the Scriptures often determine what people believe. The Roman Catholic Church maintains that the Bible is not sufficient for understanding Christian truth. The church has the task of explaining what the Bible means, and church tradition is to be regarded as one of the sources of revelation. Protestants "protested" against such a view and defended a *sola scriptura* position—the Bible alone was to be the basis for our doctrinal views. Yet it is clear that traditions have gradually also assumed a significant role in Protestant thought.

What about Adventism? Has the Adventist Church been able to stay clear of human traditions? Or is the creation of traditions unavoidable? Are traditions perhaps all right, as long as they do not go against the teachings of the Bible? We must face the undeniable fact that a religious community cannot function without traditions. Every religious community has originated within a certain context and thus is "born" with certain traditions. The Adventist pioneers found themselves influenced, at least to some extent, by the traditions of the communities from which they emerged. They were steeped in the traditions of the frontier which they followed as it moved westward. We cannot understand Ellen White apart from some Reformist traditions of nineteenth-century America. Nor can we understand Adventism today without some knowledge of the traditions of the country in which it originated and developed. And, just as surely, the traditions of the countries in which it has since gained a foothold will further influence Adventism.

It goes, however, further than this. A community shares a set of views and thereby establishes its identity. It finds itself in trouble if it no longer has a sense of common identity. When diversity has so greatly replaced its original self-understanding, an identity crisis will develop. Undoubtedly examples of this trouble present-day Adventism. But a community is not just centered on a set of fundamental beliefs. A religious community is also characterized by its rites and customs, by its mode of worship, by its particular ways of reading the Bible, and certainly also by its particular use of religious symbols and language. Let me give a few examples: To a Seventh-day Adventist "the three angels' messages," "the spirit of prophecy," "the remnant," and "the latter rain" are familiar terms and phrases. But the Calvinist terminology regarding the subtleties of the doctrine of predestination are not part of the Adventist jargon. Adventists know what to do when the "ordinance of humility" takes place, but have, as a rule, no inkling what role icons play in Orthodox worship. When Adventists read the Bible, they pay particular attention to texts that may further strengthen their view of the Sabbath or the Second Coming, but may gloss over those texts about the covenant that some Protestants would regard as providing support for the idea of infant baptism. A familiarity with the comments provided by Ellen G. White frequently shapes the way Adventists read and explain the Bible.

Sharing these and other traditions is part of what it means to be a community. What must set us apart from others is that we must continue to cultivate a willingness to critically compare the traditions of others as well as our own traditions with the Bible and must continue to be as open and unbiased as we can as we seek to gain an ever-deeper understanding of God's Word. But that is not as easy as it sounds. Once we have established certain views and theories, it becomes ever more difficult to look at all the evidence afresh, and, if need be, to change a long-cherished idea. It has been the genius of Adventism, however, that it was able to do that as it grew into the worldwide missionary movement that it is today. It will be one of the great challenges not to lose that tradition of readiness to change and to adapt as "more light" comes our way.

Again: what is the church?

When we use the word "church," we often do so with regard to a building or the organizational structure. It is important to note that one can employ the term *ekklesia* in a number of ways, much as we do the word "church" today (except that in the Bible it never refers to buildings). *Ekklesia* may refer to the universal church (e.g., Eph. 1:22; 3:10, 21; 1 Cor. 10:32), but also to a local church (e.g., Rom. 16:1; Rev. 2, 3), or to a local assembly (e.g., 1 Cor. 1:18; 14:19) or even a house church (e.g., Rom. 16:5; 1 Cor. 16:19). As already noted, the noun *ekklesia* stems from the Greek verb *kalein*, which means "to call." This calling includes a summons to relationship and mission, but also a being called together for community and, eventually, for a shared future inheritance.

The New Testament employs a variety of striking metaphors to characterize the church. Always remember that metaphors do not provide exhaustive analytical descriptions, but are catchwords that focus on one particular aspect of a given phenomenon. We must not play the various metaphors off against each other. They each emphasize one particular aspect. *Together* they help us grasp, to some extent, the complete picture.

Scripture, for instance, describes the church as a *family*, a *pillar*, a *fortress*, and an *army*. The "brother" and "sister" language that is part of the Adventist tradition has, of course, its basis in the family metaphor (e.g., Heb. 2:11). The army metaphor (see, e.g., 2 Cor. 10:3-5) is closely connected with the more extended imagery of spiritual life as a battle against demonic powers, which believers must fight with appropriate spiritual weaponry (Eph. 6:10-18).

One of the other prominent metaphors for the church is that of *the body of Christ*. It stresses the *unity* (organizational and spiritual) of the church in a unique way and places special emphasis on the *interrelatedness* and *interdependence* of the members. The members have widely differing functions, but must cooperate, and none can be discarded. The body metaphor clearly also implies the possibility and need for spiritual growth. Speaking of the church as the body of Christ provides powerful language, but we should stop short of fully identifying the church with the risen Christ and making the church a reincarnation of Christ. The church cannot exist separately from Christ, but Christ—as the second person of the Godhead—is distinct from the church. Christ is perfect, while the church, as long as it is in this world, will remain imperfect.

The metaphor of *the church as the bride of Christ* focuses on the aspect of *intimacy* and *love*—on the closest possible relationship. One might say that the body metaphor is pressed to its most extreme point in this representation of the church as having become one flesh with Christ in the marriage union with Him. The Old Testament prophetic image of Israel as God's spouse springs, of course, to mind (see, for instance, Isaiah 54:5-7). On the other hand, Scripture often describes idolatry as an adulterous relationship in which the people have replaced the bride with prostitutes. The early chapters of the book of Hosea provide the most striking example of such imagery. Remember that in the history of the church the bridal image has sometimes been loaded with ideas that go far beyond their intended application. For example, medieval women, at times, introduced strong sexual sentiments into their relationship with the Bridegroom.

Then we have the metaphor of *the church as God's temple*. The people of the Old Testament thought of the sanctuary as the place where God "lived" among His people. The antitype of such symbolism is both the heavenly sanctuary and the divine presence in the New Jerusalem, the ultimate habitat of the redeemed (Rev. 21:3). While we are still on this earth, the church is the holy temple of the Lord (Eph. 2:21). In a derived sense the individual believer is also described as a temple of God (1 Cor. 6:19, 20). What better terminology could there be to portray the church as a sanctified place in which God wants to be present?

The temple metaphor has a number of extensions. During His earthly ministry Jesus said that the Jerusalem Temple was to be destroyed, but would be rebuilt after three days (Mark. 14:58). Jesus spoke of His own work as replacing the Jerusalem Temple in the plan of God. The literal Temple—the traditional center of the worship of God—was to be replaced by a new temple that Jesus was building—a temple constructed not of stones, but of the members of the new Israel. Interestingly, Revelation 21:2 links the two metaphors together. God's people are described in one and the same breath as the holy city and as a beautiful bride adorned for her husband.

Finally, we should mention the metaphor of *the church as the people of God*. God always had, and always will have, a group of people that are His in a special sense (see, e.g., 1 Peter 2:9, which echoes Exodus 19:5, 6). Scripture also calls the people of God *saints*. That does not mean they are super-pious or near perfect. But He has set them apart from other peoples to be His witnesses. They have been "redeemed," purchased by the Redeemer, who paid for their redemption with His blood (Ex. 15:13, 16; Acts 20:28).

The priesthood of all believers

Protestants further define the church as the *priesthood of all believers*. The churches of the Reformation rediscovered this truth and emphasized the superiority of the biblical view over the sacerdotal system of the medieval church, which preached a sharp distinction between a priestly hierarchy and the "ordinary" believers, who depended for access to God on the priests as their mediators. The new people of God do not have a priesthood in their midst, as did Israel in Old Testament times. The letter to the Hebrews points out that a new and "better" ministration, with Jesus Christ as the perfect high priest has replaced the old sanctuary services. He is the one and only mediator (1 Tim. 2:5). All members of the church (men and women) are priests (Rev. 1:6; 5:10; 20:6). Baptism is the ordination to the priesthood, in which all believers share (1 Peter 2:9, 10). The New Testament refuses to make any qualitative distinction between clergy and laity. The church appoints people who have special responsibilities, but the differences between those functionaries and the other members is not that they relate to God in a more direct way. All have, through their prayers, equal access to God. All depend in the same way on the intercession of the great High Priest. And all share in the same way in the mission of the priesthood, to "mediate" (in the sense of communicate) the message of redemption to the world.

MISSION 13

"Always be prepared to give an answer to everyone who asks you to give the reason for the hope that you have. But do this with gentleness and respect."

—1 PETER 3:15, NIV

In the previous chapter we looked at what the church is. Now we will focus on what the church is for. Do we need the church? Yes, we replied. God wanted the church. Who then are we to say that we do not want it? Now we will look in some more detail at the mission of the church, that is, on why the church is needed. It exists for a number of reasons. It provides us with encouragement and support. The community of believers administers the gift of baptism and allows us to come together for the unique experience of partaking of the Lord's Supper. And it gives us the opportunity to worship with others. But in this chapter we will focus on just one aspect—the church is needed for mission.

We can define the word "mission" in various ways. Every organization—whether for profit or not-for-profit—that tries to go with the times summarizes its goals in a so-called mission statement. At times this can be no more than a gimmick. Directors and the staff are supposed to spend time together for team building and brainstorming, and formulating a mission statement is an obligatory part of the exercise. Once they have agreed upon such a statement and the board has voted it, it often never gets looked at again. That is, however, not to say that there are no exceptions. There are instances in which a mission statement serves as a constant point of reference and as the definitive guideline for all further policy development. Some organizations truly have a mission and know what it is.

But mission has a special meaning when used in the context of the Christian community. There it describes the specific task that God has committed to the church—that is, to the community to which Christians belong, and to you and me personally as individual members of the body of Christ. The task is to share the good news of Christ, which the Christian community has embraced, with all others, near and far, who also need to hear it.

In all honesty Christians must admit that the church has not always placed the highest priority on the execution of its mission. Often the church has simply operated in a maintenance mode, and has been busier with its own internal business, power plays, and survival strategies than with the urgency of building the kingdom of Christ. During long periods of its existence the Christian church did not devote its full energy and primary resources to the preaching of the gospel in "all the world." The worldwide missionary enterprise, as we know it today, dates largely only from the nineteenth century.

And what about the Seventh-day Adventist Church? Seventh-day Adventists are eager to describe themselves as a mission-driven community. That may to a large extent be justified. But let us, at the same time, not forget that it did take a few decades before the Adventist Church had a clear vision about the extent of its missionary calling, and that the missionary spirit has had its ups and downs. The history of Adventist missions shows that the church experienced the greatest missionary drive in the 1920s. Today the church is still growing (in some areas even by leaps and bounds), but in many places it no longer focuses on its mission in quite the same way it did almost a century ago. Today the church actually devotes a much smaller percentage of its income and personnel to extending its presence into "unentered" territories than it did in those days. Fortunately, it is also true that initiatives like Global Mission (started in 1990) have contributed much to a more positive trend in the Adventist missionary enterprise.

Mission not yet completed

God cannot yet give the signal "mission completed." This applies to the Christian mission in general as well as to the specific witness of the Seventh-day Adventist Church. Much has already been accomplished. The increase in the absolute number of Christians around the world is encouraging—from roughly a half billion in 1900 to just more than 2 billion now. The increase in the number of Bible translations is also a matter of great satisfaction. The Bible is easily the most translated book in the world. It is found it its entirety or in part in 2,355 of the approximately 6,500 languages that exist, and some additional 600 translation projects are currently under way.

The Bible is, in theory, available in whole or in part to roughly 98 percent of the world's population. That does not mean, however, that almost all people in the world (if they are literate) do actually read the Bible. And the mission of communicating the Christian gospel is far from completed. The world population increases at a dramatic rate, and statistics tell us that while the absolute number of Christians grows steadily, the *percentage* of Christians in the world has remained rather static for quite some time—at a little more than 30 percent of the world population. That should worry us. In spite of the enormous resources of all Christians collectively (their accumulated income has been estimated at more than $16 trillion); in spite of a total of 3.6 million Christian congregations worldwide; in spite of hundreds of missionary organizations that employ more than 300,000 missionaries, and in spite of the advanced print and audiovisual media now available, the Christian message is still not heard in hundreds of millions of homes around the globe.* Roughly one in every four people on this planet, it is estimated, has never ever heard of the Christian God and is totally unaware of who and what Jesus Christ is. About 2 billion people alive today have not yet had the opportunity to choose for or against the Christian God. How can that be? If the Coca-Cola organization can acquaint virtually all people around the world with its product, what's wrong with the 3.6 million Christian congregations and their 2 billion members? Why haven't they yet reached every city, town, and village in the world with their product? Why do thousands of "people groups" still remain unreached by the gospel?

We arrive at similar conclusions when we look specifically at the Adventist missionary enterprise. The church has done much. It has grown from a handful of people about one and a half centuries ago to a movement that will soon have a few dozen (or more) million members, spread over virtually all countries in the world. Reading the annual statistics causes one to marvel at what God has done through the Adventist community. And, in fact, Adventists may have by comparison succeeded a little better in accomplishing what they set out to do than Christianity in general. While the ratio of Christians to the world's population has remained static, there is now one Adventist to every 468 people in the world, while only 50 years ago the ratio was one to more than 3,000! But even so, we have no reason for complacency, for the Great Commission continues to challenge us as much as before.

A divinely ordained task

The English word "mission" derives from the Latin *mittere*, "to send." Mission has to do with the One who sends, those who are being sent, and the purpose for which people are sent. To be sent implies the willingness to go, which often means the crossing of various borders: physical, ethnic, linguistic, or cultural. Such mission is no divine afterthought, and in a sense is not even contingent upon the arrival of sin and the need for salvation, but is rooted in the nature of God. The Creator who wants people to relate to Him, He is outgoing. He is the Light (1 John 1:5), and is not withdrawn or absent. And He is Love (1 John 4:8,16) and therefore seeks relationships and wholeness.

Mission is a dominant theme in the Old Testament. Genesis 1-11 relates God's missionary effort to deal with the human race as a whole. Theologians have often called Genesis 3:15 the protoevangelium, the foundational message that underlines the fact that salvation will be available for all.

Later God summoned Israel to be a missionary people. The blessings of God's covenant with His people were to be universal

135

(see, for instance, Gen. 12:1-3; Ex. 19:5, 6). He definitely included the other nations in His plan as the stories of Jonah, Esther, Ruth, Naaman, etc., clearly indicate. Israel was, in a sense, a collective priesthood (Ex. 19:5, 6). It was to care for strangers (Ex. 12:48; 22:21; Num. 9:14; 15:14; Deut. 1:16; 31:12, 10). The Old Testament stresses the universality of God's purposes. The true God leaves no room for other gods or for mixtures of the true religion with aspects of paganism.

In the New Testament the emphasis on mission is even more pronounced. Christ is the supreme missionary. The Father sent Him (John 17:18, 21), yet He came voluntarily (Mark 10:45; Phil. 2:6-8). Although Israel is still very much in the picture (Matt. 15:24; 10:5, 6), the wider aspect is predominant: God so loved the *world* (John 3:16). Christ ministered therefore to people of all kinds of backgrounds and His teachings constantly emphasized the universality of the gospel message, with the missionary mandate *to go in all the world* as its climax (Matt. 28:18-20; Mark 16:15, 16; Luke 24:46-49; John 20:21, 22; Acts 1:8; 26:13-18). The book of Acts continues with a concise survey of early mission history, starting with Pentecost and spanning a few decades following Christ's departure from earth. The mission theme is also always present in the Epistles, sometimes explicit, sometimes more implicit.

The uniqueness of Christianity

Getting involved in missions makes sense only if it creates a difference, whether one does or does not preach the message of Christ. An ongoing debate, even among Christian theologians, continues about the status of Christianity among the various world religions. Three main positions have emerged. According to those who defend *pluralism*, God reveals Himself in all religious traditions. They see every religion as providing a road to the beyond, in its own historically and culturally conditioned way. If this is true, and all religions are of equal value, why persuade adherents of other world religions to become Christians?

Then there is the concept of *universalism*. Those who defend this idea focus on a number of biblical passages that appear to stress the universal impact of divine grace. A favorite passage is 1 Corinthians 15:28: "When he has conquered all things, the Son will present himself to God, so that God, who gave his Son authority over all things, will be utterly supreme over everything everywhere." Other oft-quoted texts are 1 Timothy 2:3, 4; Romans 2:6-16; 1 John 2:2; Romans 5:12-19; and Philippians 2:9-11. Advocates of universalism, however, do not take into account the clear passages that emphasize other aspects of God's interactions with humanity. Those texts that speak about damnation, for instance, get played down and explained as merely hyperbolic. Some universalists believe that those who have not chosen rightly in this life will have a postmortem chance. They cite the statements in 1 Peter 3:18-20; 4:6 (about the "spirits in prison") in support.

Finally, there is the position of *exclusivism* or *restrictivism*. This theory defends the view that salvation comes only through Christ. People need to hear the gospel and must respond. No other name than that of Christ, they say, brings salvation. The most popular texts in support of this view are: Acts 4:12 ("There is no other name in all of heaven [except the name of Christ] for people to call on to save them"); John 14:6; Mark 16:16; and 1 Timothy 2:5. If some people will be saved without having had the chance to hear the full gospel, it will—whether they realize it or not—be through the merits of Jesus Christ. One cannot escape the conclusion, however, that ultimately some people will be lost, and that somehow the church's missionary effort does make an eternal difference.

Adventists are among those who believe that, when one considers and weighs all the biblical data, the only defensible view is the last one. If all religions were equally valid, a fully secular worldview would be just as acceptable. Adventists defend the uniqueness of Christianity because of the uniqueness of its founder: Jesus Christ. They acknowledge the similarities between most of the world religions, but also insist there are crucial differences between Jesus and the founders of other religions. No other religious founder ever claimed to be the eternal Creator-God, assured us that He is able to forgive sins, or rose from the dead. The main criterion is not whether a religion satisfies its adherents. We cannot casually brush aside the truth claim. It does not mean that all non-Christian religions are totally bad and that we cannot learn anything from them. But since the various religions make mutually incompatible claims about reality, they cannot all be true at the same time.

The uniqueness of Adventism

Adventists insist that Christianity is unique among the world religions, but will also want to be sure that their faith has a unique status within Christianity. We need to especially consider two aspects.

First, Seventh-day Adventists do not believe that they are the only agents in God's plan for the salvation of humanity. Since 1926 the following paragraph has been in the *General Conference Working Policy*: "We recognize those agencies that lift up Christ before men as a part of the divine plan for the evangelization of the world, and we hold in high esteem Christian men and women in other communions who are engaged in winning souls to Christ." Adventists see themselves as key players in the end-time missionary thrust. Mission is a major part of their reason for existence, but they also see a role for others.

Second, Adventists could understand their movement basically in three different ways: 1. The Adventist Church is the true church—other churches are false. Adventists, therefore, are the only true witnesses and conduct the only true Christian missionary work. 2. The Adventist Church is just one segment of Christianity—it is one serious option among many other valid options. It is not so important that Adventists themselves reach people, but rather that the Christian message in some form or another touches them. 3. Adventists do not claim to be the only ones involved in Christian mission, but present a Christian option that offers a number of insights not readily available elsewhere and that correct certain widely held erroneous opinions. They place special emphasis on certain neglected, but essential, scriptural truths. In other words, Adventism makes a vital contribution to the richness of Christianity. This third view describes what Adventism "officially" believes.

Giving the gospel hands and feet

The mission outreach of the Adventist church has two focal points: the preaching of the gospel as understood by Seventh-day Adventists, and a practical extension of the power of the gospel in humanitarian and social work. This second aspect is not a mere appendix, but an indispensable part of the church's mission.

Through the centuries the Christian church has played a major role in caring for the sick and the poor, for orphans and widows, etc. Gradually, in most Western countries the secular state has assumed many of those responsibilities and the church has largely withdrawn from this domain. At times, we should also recognize, there has been a lack of balance. Liberal Protestantism has had the tendency to emphasize the kingdom of God in purely earthly terms and to reduce the good news to a purely "social gospel." Many evangelical denominations, on the other hand, have long hesitated to get involved in humanitarian services.

What was true for evangelicalism in general has only to some extent been true of the Adventist Church. The "health work" started quite early, and the establishment of health institutions became a regular factor in the organizational development of Adventism. Dorcas societies became a fixed feature of local congregations, and "community work" became a more important aspect of Adventist outreach after World War II. The church established the Seventh-day Adventist Welfare Services (SAWS) in 1956, while the Adventist Development and Relief Agency (ADRA) evolved from SAWS and has grown into a worldwide humanitarian network

Some Adventists still argue that the church should invest all its energy in preaching "the truth," since "time is short." Fortunately, there exists a fairly wide consensus in the Adventist Church that the church's mission has a twofold dimension of preaching and serving, although there has hardly been any attempt to define the various aspects of the mission outreach in theological terms.

In the language of the people

The issue of contextualization is of paramount importance in the worldwide community that carries out its mission in some 200 countries. Contextualization is a biblical principle. The gospel must be preached in terms that the listeners can understand. The Old as well as the New Testament show that the cultural *forms* were constantly *adapted* to package the *unchanging content* of the divine message. Christ gave the great example when He came in human flesh, and assumed a form that we could identify with. Today the search for culturally relevant forms remains a must if the message is going to be heard and understood.

Traditionally Christian theology has been the domain of Western *men*. It is not only legitimate, but absolutely necessary that *women*, and people from *non-Western* cultures increasingly do their part in translating the Christian message for the population groups they represent. Any contextualization must never compromise with the pure content of the message. *Syncretism* (an uncritical mixture of elements from different cultures and religions, such as we find in the New Age movement) is unacceptable.

There must be a critical contextualization in the use of evangelistic methods and in the use of the language and images employed to explain the core meaning of Christian teachings. The same is true for the various ways in which people around the world worship. If we ignore this process, the message will remain foreign to the people that are the target of the mission outreach. The resulting diversity in the church is not a threat to its unity, for true unity does not demand uniformity.

Living our mission

Witness is a community enterprise. It needs vision, leadership, strategies, organization, resources, training, and—you name it. But when everything is said and done, it is also a personal matter. The "church" can do only certain things, if you and I do them. The gospel can be preached only if you and I are willing to go out, cross cultural barriers, and give account of our faith and hope in Christ. The power of the gospel will become visible only if you and I demonstrate what Christ can do in human beings who surrender to Him.

As always, there is a price tag. We may translate the Greek word *martyros* as "witness," but also as "martyr." That in itself already indicates that choosing Christ may be a costly business. Many Christian witnesses have paid the ultimate price in Bible times and throughout history, and even in today's world there exist many places in which professing Christ is a risky business. Its should not come to us as a surprise, for Christ did not leave us without warning. "If any of you wants to be my follower, you must put aside your selfish ambition, shoulder your cross, and follow me" (Matt. 16:24). If you do, it is fully worth it, for "if you give up your life for me, you will find true life" (verse 25).

Being a witness is our mission. It is more, however, than holding a church office, supporting the community to which you belong with your finances and influence, or even knocking on doors. Our mission will shape our complete lifestyle and all our relationships. Becoming the light of the world and the salt of the earth (Matt. 5:13-16) affects our attitudes and our ambitions, and everything we have, are, and want to be.

---

* A number of specialized agencies collect such statistics. A good, annually updated source is the *International Bulletin of Missionary Research*, from which I have taken these.

WHY DO WE NEED GOD WHEN WE SEEM TO HAVE ALL WE NEED?

Seven Reasons Why Life Is Better With God

Nathan Brown

Christianity is often styled as an answer to our problems, particularly for those who have no options left. But what about those who seem to have everything going for them? who are well off, well fed, well educated, faced with many different opportunities, and apparently doing OK?

The truth is that we don't have to hit rock bottom to need God. This book ponders seven reasons life is better with God—when things are bad, God can make them better; when things are good, God makes them better still. 978-0-8127-0436-5. Paperback, 160 pages.

3 WAYS TO SHOP

- Visit your local ABC
- Call 1-800-765-6955
- www.AdventistBookCenter.com

REVIEW AND HERALD ®
PUBLISHING ASSOCIATION
Since 1861 www.reviewandherald.com